Out of Our Past Lives

Out of Our Past Lives

Elizabeth Léonie Simpson, Editor

iUniverse LLC
Bloomington

OUT OF OUR PAST LIVES

iUniverse books may be ordered through booksellers or by contacting:

iUniverse LLC
1663 Liberty Drive
Bloomington, IN 47403
www.iuniverse.com
1-800-Authors (1-800-288-4677)

Because of the dynamic nature of the Internet, any web addresses or links contained in this book may have changed since publication and may no longer be valid. The views expressed in this work are solely those of the author and do not necessarily reflect the views of the publisher, and the publisher hereby disclaims any responsibility for them.

Any people depicted in stock imagery provided by Thinkstock are models, and such images are being used for illustrative purposes only. Certain stock imagery © Thinkstock.

ISBN: 978-1-4917-3156-7 (sc)
ISBN: 978-1-4917-3157-4 (e)

Library of Congress Control Number: 2014906742

Printed in the United States of America.

iUniverse rev. date: 04/24/2014

Acknowledgements

Many people have contributed to this book. Most important of all are those latest residents of the Saratoga Retirement Community in Saratoga, California whose stories are shared here.

Judith Corney and Margaret White have spent precious time proof-reading the completed manuscript. Several avid practitioners offered good photographs for the cover; Bill Friedrichs' colorful view was selected.

This collection could not have been assembled without the continual, comprehensive assistance of my step-son, Peter Wurr, who shares a quite incredibly close relationship with my computer.

To the Reader Pray then, take care, that tak'st my book in hand, To read it well; that is, to understand.

Ben Jonson (1573-1637)

Contents

Reader's Guide

Reader, who are we who live in this beautiful, accessible retirement community? The simple answer is: a diverse lot. Are you familiar with your neighbors? We have come to know each other by dining, walking, exercising (in the pool and out), game-playing, busing to theater, concerts, and lectures, as well as through committee participation. But how well are we acquainted? Should we not know each other better? Do I have the skill and the power to guide you into this somewhat alien territory?

I would like to think that I am a modern Scheherazade, not one spinning her tales to entertain a powerful, threatening ruler and save her life. Still, I have other, inclusive reasons for putting this book together. My collection, I like to think, has been made with many, possibly equally, positive motives. These books, now three including this one, are intended for all of us to be doorways into inner, private rooms decorated by every writer and shared by all who care to enter. Here are memories we have lived with for, if I want to understand who I am today, I need to know who I was in the past.

Recollection provides identity, discovery, not comparison or even a report of reality. What it brings is an orderly reconstruction of the past, something requiring negotiation, not a microcopy, that is so individual that we may never know which part of it is true or which part of it is false. Sometimes when the writer sits down to record a personal history it comes out rushing like a commercial truck on a superhighway. We must halt the rush and select questions to ask the driver such as, should only what is praising or profitable be shared with others? What about the frightening, penetrating events that have shaped our way of thinking? Of behaving? Some happenings are subject to abandonment like an unwanted orphan child but they are part of the richness we own.

Is this type of neglect the outcome of faulty memory or deliberate distortion? Do records of the self have to be entirely true? *Can* they be? Is it possible for the person to select out what he or she would like to remember? Images in the mind come accompanied by captions learned in the social world. They supply the need for order, continuity, and consistency. The best recollections are both ambiguous and confusing and therefore open to interpretation by the person who has them. In short, perhaps that which is remembered needs to be authentic, but not necessarily accurate.

We pursue reality without any real hope of catching up with it entirely. And as we encounter its shadow and its light, we alter our perceptions and our selves are re-made. Memory is a singular construction taken from what matters to each of us. It is not an unaltered videotape, a fixed copy passed from human to human but, rather, a unique creation that is the outcome of millions of recorded sources. The social cohesion needed in any group is ornamented by recurring individuality.

Our past comes with us wherever we go, but it is not necessarily presented as front page news. Nor should it be. We have an enduring privilege in the right of choice, of selection, in how we present ourselves to others, when and where. The truth is that the memory behind that selection is the equivalent of a visit to a flea market laid out not wholly but in multiple parts, to be picked over and examined. Subject to the deterioration of time, its aspects may be invested with imagination or shaped by selective erosion. Flea markets are laden with memories. These gathered bits and pieces of arts and crafts are genuine, not attempts to imitate or outdo the lives of others. For Chinese scholars, the importance of preservation of the past was built into a proverb: *The palest ink is better than the best memory.*

The need to keep something of our past originates less in the brain's work than in that of the heart's translucent recreation, embracing what we have been and done. Memory is the mortar between events of experience, providing evidence that something happened—indeed, whether it did or not. We have the right to be the novelists of the self—a right José Ortega y Gasset called "ontological privilege."

By necessity, any writing or thinking about the past is done *a posteriori*. The writer is the present person, not the one being described imaginatively. Nor was the thinker ever exactly that person. Memory alone cannot be held to account for what is reproduced upon the written page in the name of personal retrospection or recall. But does it matter? Is it always important for the reader or the listener to know whether the tale constructed is a conscientious report, an embroidered or exaggerated truth, or an interesting but misleading story?

Retrospection is a powerful force—if it is healthy and sound and if it is given the opportunity for expression. Sharing memories as, for example, when biography or autobiography serve as acts of remembrance, accomplishes what other, more transient, forms of memorial never can: the preservation of a vanished life. Such a rendering endures as a monument, evocation, explanation, and summary. But, although the package may be closed, it is still accessible for revision at a later date.

Sharing memories in person, agreeing on the grand image of the past, as friends, family, or the members of a larger society have always done, is a comforting, self-validating process. Memory is more than an ornament; it is a necessary part of the structure of the human organism. It permits the individual not simply to travel in time but to play on the past as if it were an accordion, expanding and collapsing it at will, altering its timbre, volume, and rhythm, together with its range of feeling. Whenever this takes place, it is neither chronology nor factual exactitude which gives importance to memory. It is meaning.

That meaning is drawn from a web of myth woven from belief and hope and applied in actions both social and personal. When conflict arises between distinct and differing realities, simple but valuable mechanisms are used to respond to the dissonance which occurs. Basic among these are the capacity to forget and its alternative, the ability to alter the past—to re-write history of the social world or the person. These may be either conscious, deliberate tactics, or unconscious ones occurring automatically through the internal defense mechanism that Sigmund Freud called "repression."

This collection of essays presents many aspects of remembering. It is a book for gourmet tasting, not the satisfaction of ravenous hunger. If you take the editor's advice, you will savor, not try to devour.

The healthy life, the valued life, is bound by three dimensions. It is a life in which every present moment holds both memory and anticipation. Past, present, and future co-exist. Each has its depth and form, but they are not necessarily sequential or linear. Living in the present alone might be like being stranded on a small island. Though its resources may be plentiful and varied, in a short time they will become too familiar, too narrow, and too restrictive. The present is here, surrounding us at all times, not to be avoided and not to be separated completely either from yesterday or the tomorrow for which hopes, plans, and expectations already exist. These properties of time merge; their boundaries are not fixed, and the individual living through them is a wanderer whose path is not entirely self-chosen. In each mind, formless moment succeeds fulfilled moment, amorphous year succeeds the reality of completed year. At life's end, the third dimension of anticipation shrinks, inevitably foreshortened by the awareness of death's imminence.

Given the wide range of backgrounds (rural and urban, American and foreign), interests, and variety of experiences, our open community—an elaborate polyglot—is available for enduring exploration. Here we are all essayists (and two are poets). Some have been physical adventurers: by canoe or hitchhiking around the world. Some have written of the meaning their careers or amateur ventures have given to their lives (the building of dams, physical therapy applied around the world, nursing, and acting.)

Many other ways of life and thinking are exhibited in these pages to inform and entertain you.

At the age of 40, an unmarried physician decided to adopt a newborn and raise him alone to maturity. The power of loved family members (especially a grandmother with a special nickname or a family farmer), friendship with a man from Washington state who became internationally famous, and the gift of money to support esthetic interests are described by those touched by these influences. Here life in small groups is explored—whether it is growing up in a Midwest farm town or becoming participant in the training of doctors in a famous clinic.

Told by those who have lived through them, not all of these accounts are completely happy ones. Scarred by fire as a child, a successful grandmother still remembers her pain and her long fear of being ignored or disliked. Smitten with cancer, a singer finds a religious message which bolsters her strength. Two women who have collected data for a book they were writing together lose a year's work on their indexed material when heaving mountains bring on a computer crash. A small boy, visiting with his parents at Niagara Falls, disappears into a crowd. (This one ends with mutual joy.)

All these tales are shared case histories, living memories and not ones that have vanished. For each of us our recollections are windows to the past, revisiting occasions that may be welcomed or rejected, clarifying, or an enduring painful, ugly blot upon nearer scenery. In all of human life, the process of remembrance has an essential dual function, both for you, the reader as well as the writer, and for society. It provides continuity in time for the thought and feeling processes of distinct, observing persons. For the individual, memory is a transaction between personal history and development. The past, as it is recalled, changes the way in which the person develops, the route taken, as well as the destination.

But memory also provides a fluctuating center for the establishment and maintenance of social groups. All such groups—families, friends, societies, and nations—have aspects of memory in common with the individuals who comprise them. In all cases, more is retained than is readily available, useful, or valued. Mechanisms of selection and repression are ours to use to cull out what is not wanted or even acknowledged and to emphasize a past which enhances the present with its possibilities for the direction or ornamentation of the future. Within nations, this process is often done at the conscious level, *e. g.,* the Japanese produced textbooks which greatly understated their role in World War II. This type of distortion is not at all exclusive to Japan; every society has a preferred collection of historical "facts" chosen to be presented and taught to forthcoming generations. Until recently, textbooks in the United States did not discuss the deceits and ravages perpetrated against native American tribes whose lands were expropriated. History books provided by the European countries described the plundering of raw materials from their colonies and their use as captive markets as bringing enlightenment, peace, and justice—a process piously known as assuming "the white man's burden."

The freedom to determine what happens next is limited at any stage of life—a limitation that becomes increasingly obvious over the passage of time. It is true, as the poet Robert Burns wrote, that "The best laid schemes o'mice and men/Gang aft a-glay'" Of the three time fields of life, it is the past alone that can be fully controlled. Why? Because it alone can be recalled and altered by the person who has lived it—the one individual who has access to those memories. He or she is the sole origin of this mental material which is unique in its entirety. Each memory is singularly selectable, available only to one person and processed completely by that one. Influences can be applied to shape or alter memories, but their effect can never be total. Remembrance within its isolated, personal cell sends tendrils into the bygone which can pull forth an entire world and form it into a believable entity, a whole created and preserved by memory's selective tools.

Intended as preparation and support, memory provides for what is to come as a record of what has already occurred. Its devices and mechanism reside in a domain which includes the mind but is not it exclusively. What the body and the mind together have learned cannot be forgotten; it can only be buried or disguised. The person *is* his or her past—even if it cannot be remembered at a conscious level. Belief in the validity of that massive, sometimes inaccessible, storage is necessary and real. Undefined, unseen, but deeply felt, that belief remains forever influencing the attitudes and motivations of the present. The past is the stage for today, the prolegomena, whether or not it is retained consciously.

Remembering should not only be a ruminative self-hypnosis but, rather, the introspection needed for new adaptive stances. It has been described by an unknown author as "that shaft on which we turn, wheeled by the past with gears of motivation and desires."

Concluding the manuscript, closing the manifold files, I—the editor—am left with a handful of words, words which slip between my grasping fingers like the brightest of winged seeds. I would like to restrain them, water, and feed them, nurture them into bud, flower, and fruit. But I cannot. They are carried by the undercurrent of air, invisible, loose, and random. Their evocative presence cannot be held, their silent tale cannot be told, just as the empty page cannot be read. One cannot remember what was never recorded, for the expaerience is lost if it is never achieved in some communicable form. But here, here in this compilation, writers of many kinds, each a sage in his or her own area of human experience, remain a well from which to draw over and over again, a source for gourmet tasting. Savor, do not try to devour.

Elizabeth Léonie Simpson, Editor

Alone by Canoe

Alan Corney

In May of 1954 I graduated from Brown University and narrowed down my job choices quickly to work in sales. I felt more comfortable selling tangibles such as things in department stores, rather than intangibles like insurance or stocks.

With no family business to go into, no money to invest, and no business experience at all, retailing seemed to be a good opportunity to gain expert guidance, as well as the experience of running a business using someone else's money. The major requirement was to work hard—which I had already been doing for the past four years in college. I had offers to join the R. H. Macy training squad in New York City, starting at $75/week or Bloomingdale's starting at $65/week and I chose Bloomingdale's. It was smaller and less likely to lose me in the shuffle. Their program seemed better focused on training future buyers and mentoring them. The surprise was that they wouldn't take me until my draft status was resolved.

The Korean war had wound down, but the draft was still in effect. I went to the draft board every week during May, June, and July that year to plead with them to call my number, but they didn't need anyone. Since I had already been rejected by the Navy, Marines, and Air Force for severe heart murmur when I tried to enlist in the ROTC at college, I was pretty sure I would be classified 4F by the draft board when they did call me. Since I didn't know how long this statement would last, I needed to get a temporary job. There weren't many available that late in the season, but I finally convinced the director of Broad Creek Scout Camps to start a canoe trip program for senior Boy Scouts. (One of my strong motives was to be able to visit Judy Robinson in Princeton, New Jersey before she entered her Senior year at Brown University.)

I was to make the first trip by myself to try out routes and plan camp sites. Since I had previously canoed the upper Susquehanna River, I decided to go some 125 miles south past Conowingo Dam into the head of Chesapeake Bay and then east through the Chesapeake and Delaware Canal to Delaware Bay. It didn't look that far on my Esso road map to go upriver to Trenton, New Jersey.

I called Judy and told her that I was on my way. I would probably be there in three days, in time for the July 4th weekend. The first night I slept on the beach at Elk Neck State Park in the western end of the canal with the luxury of hot showers. I don't know why it took so long the next day to get 21 miles to the eastern end of the canal, but I was still paddling after dark. I think it was almost midnight when I got to the control station. I was very tired and out of drinking water. That was when I heard a ripple in the water, but couldn't see anything around me. I thought there might be a muskrat in the water but I couldn't see one. When I heard it again I looked all around, even upward. I saw a little red light about 40-feet almost directly above me. What I was seeing suddenly hit me: I was looking at a cigarette held by the lookout on the bow of a freighter coming right up behind me! It was steam-powered and much quieter than diesel-powered ships. I dug out of there in a panic and missed the crest of the bow wave by a couple of feet. Not much later I tied up at a rickety old dock and rolled out my sleeping bag on the grass in front of the control station. That was a night I remember! I had been raised on rivers and lakes and had no experience in tidal waters.

Starting up the Delaware River, by the time I got to Wilmington I was making almost no headway against the current and the outgoing tide. Exhausted, I grabbed onto a large mooring buoy and held on to catch my breath. Then a small outboard motorboat coming up the river also tied up to the buoy for the pilot to refill the gas tank on top of his outboard motor. Stopping periodically was necessary because that was before the days of large tanks connected to the boat's motor by a rubber hose. The stranger was struggling upriver in a 14-foot wooden boat with a small engine by today's standards. I think he was reluctant to tow me, but my forlorn condition changed his mind.

Coming up to Philadelphia I was back on my own and kept to the east of the large island in the middle of the river. That brought me along the docks of Camden, New Jersey and two huge signs on industrial buildings for RCA and Campbell's

Soup. Up ahead I could see a rowboat in the river with no one in it. As I got closer, I saw a hand come up from the other side of the boat and drop something into it. Going even closer, I found two young men retrieving items from the river bottom. They told me that they were anchored over a collapsed Campbell's pier, and were retrieving canned goods that had been stacked on the pier. Because the water had loosened all of the labels, it wasn't practical for the company to try to salvage the load, but these fellows didn't care whether it was soups, vegetables or anything else. They were going to eat it.

Later in my trip I paddled until long after dark and pulled up on the river bank to sleep. It must have rained during the night because I woke up in a wet sleeping bag. Getting there had taken longer than expected and I was out of food and water. There were some kids having a swim nearby, and they took me up to their house to get a long drink and fill my canteen. This turned out to be the hottest weekend of the summer. By then Judy was beginning to wonder if I was really coming to visit her. She called my mother in Baltimore, unfortunately, who—since I had left three days earlier—went into a panic. All during that long hot July 4th weekend everyone, including my parents, was very worried about my safety and my whereabouts. All were greatly relieved when I arrived safely in Trenton, even though dehydrated, sunburned, and totally exhausted.

While Judy's family was impressed with my paddling a canoe upriver and against the tides for approximately 125 miles, they also wondered how wise it was to travel a dangerous path by myself and whether I should be taken seriously as a husband and future father. By early afternoon of the holiday I had reached Trenton and called Judy. There was no answer since that was before the age of home answering machines. Judy had been sitting indoors for three days waiting for me to call until her parents finally dragged her out to have a holiday dinner with them. I did reach her later that day and she and her Dad drove into the city to pick me up.

After I had a shower, Judy's mother, Marion, started bringing me hot tea, about three kettles full. Since I never needed to pee, we knew that I had been seriously dehydrated. That night I slept on the living room sofa and, when I started to wake up, I had a strange experience. I could see two fish swimming above me, but I was breathing air. How could that be? I finally realized that I was looking at two paintings of fish on the fireplace mantle above my head.

Judy went off to work as a secretary at the RCA Research Lab so Marion brought me several glasses of orange juice before she left for her office. I slept until she woke me when she came home for lunch. A couple of nights later Judy drove me into Trenton to catch a bus home to Baltimore. While waiting in the station, we had our first conversation about what it might be like for us to be married. I had already been told as a teenager that it was unlikely I would live past 50, or 60 years at the most. Could she manage living as a widow for 15 or 20 years? The foolish girl said, "Yes!" That summer I led several canoe trips for senior Scouts on the Susquehanna River. In early August I raided my piggy bank and bought a maroon 1950 Ford convertible for $400 so I could get to Princeton to visit Judy. The doors didn't lock; the top didn't retract; the radio was missing; and the muffler sounded like an 18-wheeler.

But it was my first car; gasoline was 19-cents a gallon, and I was thrilled to have it. Finally, at the end of August I got my draft notice to take the pre-induction physical. The doctor, holding his stethoscope to my chest, called over one of his buddies, "Listen to this one. It sounds like a tin can." As I had expected, my future would not include service in the Armed Forces. The first week of September I started the Bloomingdale trainee program and realized right away that a car in New York City was a liability. I sold the car for $425. The increase just about covered the cost of the two new tires I had bought.

A Kansas Beginning

Lou Yabroff

I was born during the Depression on a very hot day in July in 1921 in the very small community, Viola, Kansas. Our town consisted of Main Street with a grocery, a drug store, a post office, a bank, and a barber shop with two Protestant churches. (The Catholic church was seven miles away.) The grain elevator we used was on the edge of town next to the railroad tracks. We were 25 miles away from Wichita, Kansas, our big city, where my grandparents lived. Our own small community had a population of around 300. We all knew our neighbors and every one of us had help from each other when it was needed.

This farming community grew mostly wheat with a small acreage of oats, barley, and corn. My father was a "dirt farmer." We always had a big vegetable garden, enough cows for milk and cream, and chickens with plenty of eggs. It was my job as a little girl to wash the eggs and put them in a 36-dozen case. Once a week Grandpa would take them into Wichita and peddle them to neighbors and the local grocery store. For my part of the work Grandpa gave me ten cents. That was my allowance! I felt so rich!

Our family of six children had three of each gender. We went to a very small school with all twelve grades in one building. Our Dad drove us there since we only had one car but a few times we had to walk about three miles. That red brick building had three floors. The basement was for Home Economics and Manual Training (for the beginning of carpentry), and the bathrooms. The ground floor held grades one through eight with three grades in each classroom. The top floor was for high schoolers. All of this space was filled by busy, active pupils from six to 18 years old.

I well remember Mrs. Orr, my first grade teacher, who was a buxom woman with a big lap. Whenever a child had a headache or an upset stomach she would hold them in her lap and give them peppermint water to make them feel better. She held children a lot!

This big red brick building had another wooden one next to it that was for sports (basketball and volleyball), dances, and community activities such as voting. At one end of this building was a large elevated stage where we did many plays and band concerts. It also served as a community space for the library and lectures.

We were a close family who had a good time growing up together. But my brothers and sisters blamed me for bringing home all the available childhood sicknesses: chicken pox, three-day and red measles, mumps, and whooping cough, as well as many colds and flu. We all joined the Four H Club at age ten and I stayed through my 17th year. This was a part of the Farm Bureau for men, as well as for women. It gave all the young people in the community a chance for leadership development because each child had responsibilities. All of us had to take classes in practical subjects and were expected to participate by giving reports to fellow students.

Those practical subjects included Home Improvement of various kinds. Some were sewing, baking, canning, and health. Clothes for myself were part of the course—a dress and slip which won prizes in the county and the state competitions. Another area of learning was the care of livestock. For me, that included a steer and a little pig for whom I paid $10. I brought the pig home held in my lap. "Penny" was his name as he was a red pig and I rubbed his skin many times with a corn cob. The animals were sold at the end of the fair. I had to keep my own expense book and show it to my Dad and my 4H leader.

When my sisters and I wanted to learn to play the piano, my mother paid our teacher with farm products such as butter or eggs. Everyone shared in a lot of ways. One of these was that, when full plates were taken to a community meeting, they went home just as full but with someone else's cooking. When we were trying to raise money for the library or other things, families decorated boxes filled with food which were bid up by the auctioneer, who was often our Dad. He was a man who loved being with people. We kids said of him that he "had never met a stranger."

Winter brought our neighbors out for ice-skating on the large pond which accumulated in the hollow by the railroad tracks. Our skates were "clamped on style" and would fit most any hard-soled shoe or boot. We had a key to make the skates stay on our shoes. If some people didn't want to skate the way we did, they might be pushed around the ice sitting on chairs or stools with runners or wheels. Logs were piled up next to the pond and a fire started where we could toast sticky, sweet marshmallows There was lots of coffee and hot chocolate.

None of this was unusual for my family or the other farm ones around us.

My older sister, Elaine, went to college for two years to become a teacher in the lower grades and then went to teach in a one-room grade school not far from where we lived. When I was 14, she became ill and couldn't teach. I piped up and said with confidence, "I can do that!" and went off and did it for her for three whole days. My Dad drove me there and built the fire in the building before he left. I had a roomful of kids! At the end of each day I felt very pleased with myself and my ability to handle that school! My sick sister gave me some "Tange" lipstick to wear so I would look grownup.

While I was still in high school, in the summers I drove the tractor for my Dad for most of our planting. That was because the boys and men who usually would have been farming were away in the war then.

In 1939, I graduated as the Valedictorian in my class of 12 students. I was given a scholarship and began attending the Methodist college in Windfield, Kansas. Southwestern College, which was both a teachers' and a preachers' college, closed on Mondays so the preachers could go from one Methodist church to another to preach in the afternoon on weekends. Southwestern was 60 miles away from my home so I only went there for the holidays. But I was still close to my family. The sheets from my twin bed went home to be washed since the college had no public laundry building. When my mother sent them back clean, there was often a surprise in the package. Sometimes it was cookies or fruit or—a real treat!—a package of gum.

My days were full. Apart from my classes and homework, I worked for my room and board by waiting on tables in the cafeteria. During my second year I was paid to grade students' papers. I did all the true or false answers; the professors did the rest.

I met my first husband, Don Smith, when we were juniors at my college. When we graduated from Southwestern, he joined the Navy and was sent to Annapolis for training. He came home to visit and we made plans. That Christmas we were married—a story that ended in tragedy, as so many did then. He died in battle at sea and I was alone for 13 years.

After I graduated I taught school in a small cattle town, Douglas, near my college. I was teaching Home EC to both junior and senior high. The senior high school boys I taught how to oil and repair our sewing machines. The male teachers were off fighting so, for the first time, the boys were being taught by us females. In our food classes we would go shopping, learning the names of much of the fresh fruit and vegetables. They had never been shopping with their mothers. We took a surprise walking trip into the local poultry shop where the owner chopped the chicken's head off and cleaned it. (My mother taught me to wring the chicken's neck. That was a messy business and I did not want to teach them that procedure.)

In Health classes we had no textbooks so I used magazines and newspapers for classroom material. Smoking was a big deal for both boys and girls in high school. I had them each go around and sniff each other. There were lots of giggles, but they agreed that it smelled bad and the majority of smokers were able to stop smoking.

When we talked about getting girls pregnant, I stressed that the boys were as responsible as the girls were. Each of them was assigned a bag of flour to carry with them at all times. This was to make them more aware of the meaning of unsafe sex. Pregnant girls had to carry the weight before the baby was born and afterwards someone had to be responsible for him or her all the time. I was a very young teacher with lots to learn, but I got the point across. The next semester our girls had to go through the same routine. Fortunately, none of them got pregnant during the two years that I taught.

What made me change my career was a series of tragedies: four deaths (my principal, my landlord, my best friend's husband, and my own husband's death in a typhoon in the Philippines). I resigned from teaching and went home to farm with my Dad. My family was very supportive, but encouraged me to look for other work. Farming was too difficult and I wasn't strong physically. Besides, I was bored.

Time passed and I moved to Topeka to work with teen age girls in the YWCA. When I was there, the competition with the Girl Scouts organization was very strong. We started a club program called the Girl Reserves and, as hard as I worked, the Girl Scout organization was too strong in the public schools. I could never match their program for the YWCA girls.

More successful with the YWCA young women who were called the Y-teens, I was selected to represent that group at an international conference in Oslo, Norway sponsored by the YWCA, the YMCA, and the World Council of Churches. Its theme was *Jesus Christ is Lord*. Some 1,500 participants came from 70 countries—all under 30 years of age. Taking a Wichita train to New York where we met the other delegates from the U.S., we boarded a ship and sailed to Europe together. Because of my Don's recent drowning, I wore my Mae West for the first half of the trip—until we were past the point of no return—and it was hot!

The conference was wonderful. Every lecture was in four languages: Norwegian, German, French, and English. We were each given the appropriate equipment to hear discussions in our own language and came away feeling that we had learned a great deal.

Afterwards I took a train to visit my Grandmother's home place in Hjo, Sweden where I was entertained royally by my cousins for four days. One of the male cousins had made the arrangements for my visit by getting in touch with a Swedish American relative. This man from Illinois accompanied me and did the necessary interpretation when I got there. Because there were no cars, we walked everywhere—to the lake, the stores, museums, and the church. One day we walked through the woods to a funeral where I embarrassed my family when one of them heard the click of my camera. I had taken a photograph of the flower-covered casket that was forbidden. What I was after was the beauty of the many assorted blooms. Another time I also learned something about Swedish cookery: all ingredients were weighed, not measured by cups or spoons! I had a wonderful, happy holiday!

Back in Topeka I gave many talks about this experience in churches and schools, trying to promote good will and peace among differing peoples. I wanted to start with the differences within my own country. My boss became jealous of my speaking requests and gave me a poor evaluation of my work. He arranged for my not having my contract renewed. Our dislike was mutual and so I went to Tucson, Arizona as the director for teen-aged girls. My students were young Indians who were only interested in swimming at the YWCA pool.

After a short time in there, I moved on to San Mateo in California to work with teenage high school girls in a local YMCA. My co-worker, who had informed me of this available job, lived in San Francisco. Her boyfriend, George, and Irv—later my husband—lived in Palo Alto. It was to be my "blind date treat": to see *Swan Lake* with them in the city and it turned out to be a wonderful evening!

After 13 years of being alone, that was the beginning of an interesting and romantic courtship!

After six months we were married. I wanted to introduce my new husband to my Kansas family in Wichita. When we landed, the doors opened on the airplane. As we were coming down the stairs, we heard a band starting to play. How nice! How welcoming! I had told Irv that he didn't know my family. They might even have hired a band to welcome him! And there they were, all lined up to greet us. It was so exciting! Little did I know that the band was playing for some big Catholic event. The priest was following us off the plane! When we looked around, there were groups of nuns waiting to welcome *him*, not *us*!

Three Very Happy Years in a Small Town

Alfreda Mastman

In 1956, my husband, Gary, received a telegram from the Mayo Clinic in Rochester, Minnesota. They asked why he hadn't responded to their acceptance of him in their Ophthalmology Department for a three-year fellowship. To this day I wonder if I could have possibly thrown out their letter by mistake. He had already been accepted for a residency in Buffalo, New York where we both were born and raised. Concerned how to handle this, nevertheless we agreed that we needed to move to Minnesota. While the doctor in Buffalo was disappointed about the acceptance by that Clinic, he was entirely understanding.

The rest is history.

I was eight months pregnant with our first child, Phil. When we arrived in Rochester in June of 1956, we rented a lovely duplex downstairs of some old friends from Buffalo. We didn't have our furniture or even a refrigerator. There was only a small sink in the basement that we put blocks of ice in, brought to us by the iceman on the back of his shoulders. I had to be especially careful going up and down those stairs to our ice sink.

We waited and a few months passed without our furniture. Finally we called the Mayflower vans in Buffalo who told us that they had our things in storage until they had a bigger load going to our area! We told them how difficult this was for us, especially our sleeping on a rented three-quarter size rollaway bed in the heat of the summer. Finally the furniture came, along with a bill that was half of what it should have been because the delivery of our things had taken such an unreasonably long time.

In spite of some hardships we had a wonderful time with our friends, Herb and Molly, who lived above us. We had barbecues and socialized constantly and they were so helpful in taking me for my checkups at the Clinic. Gary couldn't do that because he was just beginning his residency while our close friend, Herb, was finishing his. Unfortunately, our friendship ended with Molly's untimely death from cancer about ten years later.

After Phil was born, we moved into a two-bedroom Quonset hut, one of a hundred huts for the residents. It had a basement where Gary had his desk to study. When he was down there, he washed clothes to drown out the noise of our, by then, two children. Mark was born two days after Paul's second birthday. We made many friends in the Eye Department (which had only 15 residents) and with our neighbors, all of whom were at the Clinic in various departments.

Coming from Buffalo, we were very used to the cold weather, but at least Rochester had sunshine during the really cold months. Temperatures in southern Minnesota were frequently 25 degrees below zero. I took the babies out for a walk even when the temperature was zero.

We were all poor in those days because the Clinic paid the residents $125 a month. The staff doctors were wonderful. The Eye Department had specialists in all phases of eye problems. People came from all over the world to get treated there. The Kohler Hotel, which housed many patients and their families, was connected through its basement to make it easier for patients in bad weather to walk right into the Clinic. The sidewalks in Rochester were heated during the long winter months. There were only small businesses around the town until IBM moved in about 1959, the year we left.

One morning I received a phone call from a neighbor who asked me if I would look outside my Quonset door to see if I could find her small white dog. It was a difficult task. The prefabs were white and there was a lot of snow out there. But she did end up finding her white dog.

Another day, when I was feeding our first son, Gary and a close friend came home and, laughing hysterically, coaxed me to go outside and look into our car trunk. They had been to a Turkey Shoot and showed me the two turkeys, complete with feathers, which they had shot. Neither one of them had ever held a gun, let alone shot anything. It had cost just five dollars to enter the Turkey Shoot, but preparing and roasting them turned out to be a big expense for us. They didn't fit in our apartment-size ovens so we had a restaurant in town clean and roast the birds for us. We had two lovely dinner parties. To this day I can remember the devilment in the two men's eyes when they showed me their catch.

One day the weather was so bad that the prefab doctors couldn't get to the Clinic to work; they were all waiting for ambulances to transport them. I was feeling a little bored and confined. To help myself to feel better, I went out to shovel snow. Gary stayed with the two little boys and baked them some frozen cherry tarts for a treat. Ah, memories, memories!

The brothers Mayo set aside some land called **Mayowood** where we could plant gardens. We had to take our own water to irrigate them, but we had fun reaping the harvest…before the ground froze.

Dr. Wilbur Rucker was a wonderful Department head. When our babies were born, he and his wife sent us baby gifts. The staff doctors lived on what we called "Pill Hill." They invited us to parties and one phone call from there was almost unbelievable. One of the staff wives invited us to stay at their home until a pending flood threat left us! Fortunately, it never happened.

When Gary had weekend call, there were at least five other residents in our neighborhood who were also on call. Many of the women and their small children gathered in our common backyard to visit and watch our children play. We got together inside a Quonset when it was too cold to be outdoors. Many of those very cold days we just stayed at home by ourselves.

The "Eye Wives" whose husbands were Ophthalmology fellows, met once a month in the evenings so our husbands could babysit. First thing on the agenda was announcing pregnancies. We planned social events and just thoroughly enjoyed visiting with each other. This group made lasting friendships.

Later on, in private practice, we lived near San Francisco where many of the "Eye Ball" conventions were held. (That was my interpretation of the Ophthalmology conventions.) It was always wonderful seeing the staff doctors, their wives, and the old residents again.

Remembering this part of our life in Rochester brings me to tears. Gary's training was incredible. Those were happy, unique years of our marriage, years in that very special small town that I will never forget.

Beverly's Hilton, I-VI

Bev and Bob Avery

PART I

Our camping experiences started in 1952 when our son was three years old and we decided he was old enough to be introduced to camping. We both loved the outdoors and wanted our children to enjoy it, too. Since Bob's maiden aunt loved the outdoors, we called her to see if we could borrow her World War I vintage tent and Coleman stove. Next, we had to decide where to go and we picked Big Basin State Park near Boulder Creek in the Santa Cruz Mountains even though it was a fair distance from Oakland in the East Bay where we lived at that time. How beautiful Big Basin was and what fun we had! We knew immediately this was the vacation lifestyle we wanted for our children and us.

Our daughter was born in 1953 and we moved from the East Bay to Los Altos in 1955 for the next six years. We continued going to Big Basin on many vacations and weekends. In those days, Big Basin was often filled up by early Friday afternoon, so late on a Thursday afternoon, in order to obtain one of our favorite camp sites, Bob would take Bev and the children over to Big Basin to set up camp. He would then return home to Los Altos to work on Friday and return to Big Basin on that afternoon. On Saturday nights we always took the children to the Ranger's campfire and nature talk with group singing. They were very educational and fun for all. In addition to Big Basin, we also camped at Bass Lake, Calaveras Big Trees, Emerald Bay State Park, Big Sur, and other public places. We loved the State Parks!

During this period, Bev noticed an ad in the Los Altos *Town Crier* for a homemade, used seven-foot long "teardrop" trailer, which became our transition to using a trailer. Its rear lifted up and disclosed a kitchen for Bev to use. She was so happy to have a kitchen while camping! It still felt like camping because she was cooking outside. Inside the trailer was great storage and our daughter used it as a playhouse. The children slept on separate cots in the old World War I tent while we slept just outside on our own folding double-bed cot that Bev had also found in the *Town Crier.*

Once, on a return trip from Big Basin, a car behind us started honking. We stopped and the driver told us that our left trailer wheel was wobbling. Bob got out the lug wrench and tightened the wheels. It would have been a major problem if one of the wheels had fallen off. The road out of Big Basin towards Saratoga is narrow with very few places to pull off, so we were lucky to find one!

Our next trailer was eight feet long with 60 square feet of living space inside. The dining table had cushioned bench seats on each side that could be made into a double bed at night. It also had a two-burner stove and an icebox. Using this trailer, we made many trips to the Pacific Northwest to visit family there. It was always a fun trip up and back—particularly not having to worry about getting wet while camping in the rainy Pacific Northwest.

In 1966 we were off to Colorado to visit family. We asked Bev's folks to join us so we rented a large tent trailer. Her folks slept on a double bed that folded out from one end of the trailer while Bev and daughter, Leslie, slept on a double bed that folded from the other end of the trailer. Bob and son, Scott, slept on cots outside. When we reached Yellowstone, Bob and Scott awoke one morning to find bear footprints alongside their cots. Fortunately, the bears must not have been hungry! Bob and Scott slept right through those visitors passing by!

PART II

In 1971, when we became "empty-nesters", we decided to buy a bigger trailer. We doubled the size of what we had to 17-foot length with 120 square feet of living space inside. Along the interior curbside of the trailer was a full-length couch (in the daytime) that folded out into a double bed at night. In the front was a dining table accommodating four people with cushioned bench seats that could also be folded out into a double bed. On the street side was the kitchen with a three-burner stove, electric refrigerator, a small sink, and counter space. In the left rear corner was a small bathroom with a flush toilet, a basin, and a shower (but with room for only one person at a time). In the middle rear was a built-in set of drawers with a small rear window above it. In the right rear corner was a built-in closet. After our more compact previous trailer, we thought we were living in a mansion! We named it "Beverly's Hilton".

From then on we were hooked on "RVing" and for the next 37 years we had a ball! At first it was trailering at least one weekend a month since Bob was still working. We found many interesting places to go that were not too far from home. While living in the East Bay, some of our favorite weekend trips were to the Mother Lode country, Carmel, and Santa Cruz. We golfed, fished, hiked, visited historical sites, and did some river rafting. But, most of all, it was the camaraderie of family and friends, sitting around a campfire at night toasting marshmallows, that we all enjoyed.

We had few problems while traveling that way, but two incidents in Arizona stand out in our memories. The first occurred near Sedona. Numerous people had told us that, while there, we should be sure to see the Chapel of the Cross located on a hillside. The view, looking down the main aisle of the church, truly framed the Sedona countryside. Since at the time we were novices at trailering, we went up the road to the Chapel and found that we could neither park nor turn around with our trailer attached. So, with Bev leading the way and guiding passing cars, Bob very slowly backed the trailer down the curving road for a half-mile where we found a side road where we could back and turn around. What seemed like hours was more likely only a half-hour or so. We were sure glad when we got to the bottom! What a lesson we learned!

The other problem we had was at Second Mesa located on the Hopi Indian Reservation in Navajo County. We had heard that it was an interesting Indian village on a hilltop. We started up the paved road with the trailer attached and halfway up there was a wide pullout beyond which the unpaved road narrowed and steepened. We asked a Hopi youngster if the road was passable for a car plus trailer and he assured us that it was. So we gave it the gas and up we went, but it got bumpier and bumpier as we went up. We stopped at the top and a group of young Hopis gathered around to inspect our vehicles. We noticed milk leaking out our trailer front door and, when we opened our front door, we found most everything from our refrigerator was on the floor. What a mess!

We got out and Bob realized that the leaf spring under the trailer had broken. The right side of the trailer had fallen and was now resting directly on the axle. What to do? The nearest town of any size was Gallup, New Mexico 120 miles away. A Hopi told us that there was a gas station at the foot of the hill on the main highway. We had little alternative but to head down the hill at a snail's pace. The attendant at that gas station told us, yes, the nearest place to get a spring replaced was in Gallup, but he was helpful and placed a wooden block between the axle and frame. He told us to go on, but at a speed of no more than 25 mph. Fortunately, since that was rather desolate country, there was little traffic. In Indian Country campgrounds were virtually non-existent so we arranged with the patrolman at the New Mexican border to sleep overnight at his station. The next day, in Gallup, we got the spring replaced and went on. This trip made us realize how beautiful the Southwest is and we returned many times during the next 37-some years.

Another month-long trip was in 1974 to Colorado where our daughter, Leslie, met us. She was on summer vacation from UCLA at the time. The three of us had a wonderful trip through Idaho that included Sun Valley and Salmon River rafting and fishing. The fishing was great and our barbecued trout dinners were wonderful! After taking in the World's Fair in Spokane, Washington, Leslie left us to fly back to her university. Both this trip and the previous one were in our 17-foot (120 sq. ft.) trailer.

While not "RVing", we kept our trailer in one of a group of horse stalls that stored farm equipment at a nearby ranch in Moraga, California. One morning, on the way to work, Bob passed by the ranch and, to his shock, he saw flames billowing from the horse stalls. Our trailer had been completely destroyed!

We immediately started to look for a replacement and found one with the same floor plan, but four feet longer (21'). We named it "Beverly's Hilton II" and did we enjoy the larger space (152 sq. ft.)! We had a larger bathroom, closet, refrigerator, and stove. We even had room for a TV. We had this trailer for seven years and slept 521 nights in it, an average of 75 nights per year. WOW! We were in heaven!

Most of our time away from home was spent on long weekends at the Pacific Coast or at Graeagle on the Feather River in the Sierra Mountains. At both places we would often leave the trailer there for several months and commute back and forth to home. During the summer months, we had many golf matches at Graeagle with our friends from home. Bev's family frequently rented a nearby condo for several weeks each summer and we had lots of game-playing, horseback-riding, hiking, and picnics. Bob enjoyed teaching our grandsons how to fish.

Our only long trip in Beverly's Hilton II was in 1982 when we were gone for eleven weeks to the East Coast. We spent many months doing the planning for that trip since Bob had business to conduct along the way. Our first stop was in Arizona to see Bev's folks who were spending a few winter months there. Then onward to Carlsbad Caverns where Bob finally talked Bev out of her claustrophobia and into descending into the Caverns. Next we went on via Austin, Texas where Bob stopped at the University of Texas, and then on into Louisiana to Avery Island and distant relatives where tabasco sauces are made. We LOVED New Orleans and spent several days there sightseeing and listening and dancing to our favorite Dixieland Jazz music. Florida was next with stops at Disney World, Cypress Gardens, the Passion Play, Cape Canaveral, and the old fort at St. Augustine.

Our first stop in Georgia was at Jekyll Island, a popular vacation stop. Next came Savannah, then westward to Americus (where Bob's mother, Elizabeth Murphey Avery, was born) and then on again to Cusseta, Georgia to visit some of Bob's distant cousins. During that time, we stopped to see the pre-Civil War home of Bob's maternal grandparents. That old house was very unusual. It had four 20-foot by 20-foot bedrooms (each with a fireplace) with two bedrooms on each side of a 14-foot wide hallway running from front to rear of the home with no doors at either end to provide better ventilation in the sweltering summer heat. A makeshift kitchen was on the back porch; the original kitchen was a brick building in the back yard where the kitchen staff also slept. We were fascinated by the floor plan of this pre-Civil War plantation home.

Next we traveled north to Pine Mountain, Georgia for a round of golf. We were staying at a trailer park that night when we noticed a little twisty symbol in the lower right corner of our TV screen. Then the TV announced that there was a tornado warning for Harris County. We didn't have any idea which county we were in but we decided to look at a map and were we unhappy to read that we indeed were in Harris County! A small RV is NOT the place to be in a tornado. It was already dark so we wouldn't be able to see an oncoming storm. We decided we could hear it coming and could go hide in the nearby empty swimming pool. Fortunately, it never arrived.

The next day Bob vaguely remembered there might be relatives in the Harris County seat of Hamilton. He decided to call his uncle in Tucson and, sure enough, he said that the Murphey family had lived in Hamilton. So we drove off to see what we could find. We really hit the jackpot!! At the courthouse there were many journals with information about the Murphey family dating back into the mid-1850s. The staff let us move the journals out of their vault to read them. A particularly interesting probate was for John Wesley Murphey (Bob's Great-Grandfather) who died during the Civil War. Among the assets listed were a spindle bed, a trundle bed, a spinning wheel, silver flatware service, a dry red cow, and numerous slaves. (At that time they were considered property.) The records also showed that the names John Wesley Murphey and Wesley John Murphey continued to be there well into the late-1900s with a final name listed as daughter Rosie Copeland.

The Murpheys were living in Hamilton long after Bob's mother's family had left, moved on to Americus, and then to Tucson in 1895. So, on a long shot, Bob looked in the local phone book, found the name Rosie Copeland and gave her a call. A lady answered and said she was Rosie and that her father and grandfather indeed were Murpheys. We were surprised to find that relatives might still be there in Hamilton, but something just wasn't adding up. Bob finally got up the nerve to ask her. "By chance, are you black?" To which she replied, "I sure am!" Apparently the Murphey family slaves had assumed the name of their owners and had remained in the same locale.

On to Oak Ridge, Tennessee and from there we went over the Great Smoky Mountains into North Carolina and on to Pinehurst for five wonderful days of golf at their famous golf courses. From there (on our way to Gettysburg) we saw many Civil War battlefields in the states of Virginia, Maryland, and Pennsylvania.

In Pennsylvania we visited the Amish country near Lancaster. We were fascinated with their rustic lives, doing without electricity, traveling with horse and wagons, and other attempts to simplify daily life. We even visited one of their homes. At nighttime, the evening silence was broken by the clip-clop of the horses and buggies as the young Amish men went courting their girlfriends.

On into New Jersey we went and stopped long enough to visit New York City and take several tours, as well as visiting the Statue of Liberty. After the hustle of the Big Apple, we were glad to be back "on the road again"—an ordinary way for RVers to express their pleasure in starting off. With our trailer on behind, we left New Jersey and went across the Verrazano Narrows Bridge to Long Island. At that time it was the longest suspension bridge in the world and gave an excellent view of the Statue of Liberty with Manhattan beyond. On Long Island Bob visited colleagues at Brookhaven National Laboratory.

The next leg of our venture was the ferry from the eastern end of Long Island to New London, Connecticut. As we docked, we saw the Navy submarine base, but leaving the ferry we had a problem. The original side mirrors on our station wagon did not stick out far enough to see around the sides of the eight-foot wide trailer so we always attached larger side mirrors to each front fender. The ferry crew had insisted that we detach the mirrors before boarding, but they would not let us reinstall them until we had disembarked. So, suddenly, we were off the ferry and onto busy city streets without any rear view capability. All we could do was use the tum signal and PRAY! Fortunately, no accident occurred and a ways down the road we were able to pull over and attach the side mirrors. What a relief finally to be able to see behind us again!

One of the main purposes of our trip had been to visit Groton, Connecticut which was just across the Thames River from New London. Bob's ancestor, Capt. James Avery, came from Devon, England in 1630 and chose to build his home there in 1656. He and his descendants lived in this place (called *The Avery Hive)* until 1894 when sparks from a passing locomotive caused the building to burn to the ground. A tall granite monument surmounted by a bust of James Avery was soon erected at the site by an Avery descendant, wealthy John D. Rockefeller.

Before we left California, we had contacted the Avery Memorial Association (of which Bob is a member) so one of the members greeted us at the Ebenezer Avery House which now is a dedicated historic home. It has been fully restored to Revolutionary War condition and moved from downtown to be next to restored Fort Griswold. The Revolutionary War Battle of Groton Heights was fought there at the Fort in September of 1781 when the traitor, Benedict Arnold, and his British troops attacked from the ocean. The locals defended the Fort gallantly, but were forced to surrender, with the wounded taken to the Ebenezer Avery house used as a hospital. Of the wounded colonial troops, more there carried the Avery surname than any other. While there, we visited nearby Mystic Seaport, a very quaint port and still home to tall sailing ships. We feasted on a New England fish lunch there.

The next day we set off for some sightseeing on our way to Boston. First we saw the mansions along the sea at Newport, Rhode Island and then we went on to Cape Cod. We stopped at Plymouth, Massachusetts where now the village has been restored completely with a full-rigged *Mayflower* and a cast of costumed colonists. But Plymouth Rock was a big disappointment. We had expected it to be boulder size, but instead we looked down into a ten-foot deep well and saw a rock hardly two feet long.

Boston was next on our itinerary and we spent several days there visiting relatives and taking in many historic sites including Beacon Hill and Old Ironsides. We also toured the famous Massachusetts Institute of Technology campus.

From Boston we headed for central New Hampshire and particularly to the small town of Marlborough near the city of Keene. This was where Bob's paternal grandmother was born and where her ancestors settled well before the Revolutionary War. We brought along a few old photos of the Tolman family home and tried driving around to find it. Since we couldn't locate it, we inquired at the local library where they referred us to the Postmaster. He, in turn, looked at the photos and said, "Yes, I recognize the house but it's gone now and the Harley-Davidson motorcycle dealership has replaced it. It was located a few miles out of Keene near the abandoned railroad tracks at Keene's Crossing." He gave us directions and we found the site and the dealership, but only a few dilapidated outbuildings were left of the family farm. How sad we were! While in Keene, we found the local cemetery and several family gravestones dating from the mid-1800s. Most of those buried there were born in the 1700s.

Next we headed west through New York state, stopping at Cornell University after which we visited the Corning Glass Works. From there on, we were headed for California and home. As we crossed over Donner Pass on our last day, we thought back over the 79 days and 8,900 miles that we had travelled. We had survived well in our 17-foot trailer (120 square feet) with no accidents or problems and had had the time of our lives. We looked at each other and said. "Shall we turn around and start the trip all over?" With big smiles on our faces. we both said. "YES!" but, unfortunately, Bob was due back at the Lawrence Berkeley Laboratory in two days.

In 1984. we decided to go even bigger and we bought a NEW 32-foot trailer (256-square feet) with every comfort, including a separate bedroom, larger bathroom, and two TVs. We thought we were in heaven again! Naturally we named her "Beverly's Hilton III". As before, we continued to go to the Monterey Bay Coast in the winter and to Graeagle and the Feather River Country in the summer.

In the summer of 1987 we were off for over a month where first we met family for a week at Jackson Hole, Wyoming. After the family left, we headed tor Glacier

National Park, then on to Waterton Lakes, Banff, Jasper, and Lake Louise in Canada. The beauty of the Canadian Rockies had beckoned us. We then headed home through eastern Oregon.

The next long trip was in the summer of 1989 when we went to eastern Canada and back. We travelled 11,288 miles and were gone 64 nights, through 26 states and five Canadian provinces. On this trip our very closest friends (neighbors from Moraga) went with us in their RV. We did most of our sightseeing separately but traveled together. At the start of the trip, our friends had already gone ahead to their hometown of Grace, Idaho to visit family and friends and we joined them there. While in Grace, we played golf on their local course. Believe it or not, the wagon wheel tracks of the Oregon Trail are still visible today.

Leaving Idaho we travelled through the northern United States and the Canadian provinces of Ontario, Quebec, New Brunswick, and Prince Edward Island. We even got as far as Nova Scotia.

It was then time to turn our trailer westward and head for home. We purposely went through Kansas where Bev's side of the family came from. Her grandparents' house in Narka, Kansas, built in 1898, was still there. (Bev had brought an old photo with her.) She also found several graves of relatives and the house in Almena, Kansas where her mother was raised. After the Kansas stops. we went straight home.

In 1990 Bob fully retired and we knew we wanted to continue RVing in our retirement. We decided that Arizona was where we wanted to spend our winters so we bought a lot in an RV Park. The park had its own nine-hole golf course, two swimming pools, four tennis courts, eight shuffleboard courts, and a Recreation Hall with a dance floor big enough for 500 people to dance or sit down at one time. Since we loved to dance and golf, the park was perfectly suited for us. About 2,000 people lived there in the wintertime. Most of the residents were "Snowbirds" from northern states and Canada who went home for the summer. As the years went by, we became very involved in some of the activities there. For example, we were in charge of the weekly dances for several years. Bev also played in Ladies' Golf. We loved the place so much that we spent 16 winters in Arizona. For ten of those, our youngest grandson (from age seven to 17) flew down to join us for a week. The three of us took in many Cactus League baseball games—especially our San Francisco Giant baseball games. Our RV resort was named "Roadhaven", but our grandson called it "Roadheaven."

While our winters were headquartered in Arizona, we took many wonderful trips throughout the southwest, most of them for golfing with friends who also had their own RVs. Our trips took us from Arizona to southern California, Nevada, and Mexico.

In 1993, we decided it was time to give up our 32-foot trailer so we bought a 28-foot motorhome (224 square feet) behind which we towed our Honda sedan. We felt much safer then. We had two drivable vehicles in case one had problems as we were often on many back roads out of cell phone range.

In 1999, we bought a 34-foot motorhome (272 square feet.) That was our biggest RV ever! We named it Beverly's Hilton V. With our Honda attached to the rear, our total length was 50 feet. Can you believe that Bev drove the rig for more than one-third of our RV travels? Since she didn't enjoy backing up, Bob always took care of that when it was needed.

In 2005, we decided to go smaller since Bev was not happy driving the large motorhome anymore. We got ourselves a 30-foot Class C motorhome that came with a cab similar to that of a van. She felt much more comfortable driving it. We appropriately named it "Beverly's Hilton VI". All of our motorhomes had queen-size beds, large shower baths, and convenient kitchens. When travelling, we barbecued often and always played dominoes (with a running score). Bev read while Bob worked many jigsaw and crossword puzzles. Wherever we went we usually had a beautiful view of either the ocean, the mountains, or the wonderful Arizona desert. Often there were trips up and down the West Coast, travelling to or from a Dixieland Jazz Festival for several nights.

Deciding that it was time for us to give up RVing, in 2009 we moved to the Saratoga Retirement Community. It was one of the hardest decisions we've ever had to make, but both of us were in our 80s at the time. At SRC we have many new activities and friends which keep us as busy as we want to be. Though we know those good days are behind us, we will always cherish our memories of over 57 years with family, friends, or just the two of us—recollections that can never be taken away.

Living Overseas as a Physical Therapist

Finding Myself in Travel and Work

Barbara Merrill

I am a physical therapist originally from New York City. I had decided in college that I wanted to live in Europe for a while. After all, my brother Tom, a physician, had spent his Junior year abroad while at Yale, so I was going to do at least as well. Since my brother had studied in Germany, I was going to do that. I made preparations expecting both to work and to study. My mother's contribution was to have me live at home. That way I could save enough money to live in Germany and its surrounding area until I started my job in England. (It's hard to believe now that my first job at the Hospital for Special Surgery in New York paid only $3,000 a year.)

A professor at Tufts University recommended Harefield Hospital in England where they specialized in chest physical therapy. (In England this is referred to as physiotherapy.) An area of physical therapy not done in the United States at the time, it is still only done on a very marginal basis. It helps prevent complications from lung and heart surgery and improves breathing for people with lung conditions. She said the work would be interesting and she found it valuable.

I applied to the University of Munich and, believe it or not, was accepted. I passed the German test—written and spoken—and the first part of my adventure was in the works.

In 1962 I boarded the ship *La France* to Paris and spent a couple of weeks with a friend who had lived with us in New York. There I could bone up on my feeble

French. I stayed, had a wonderful time with her family, and went with her through southern France to Spain. We did all the tourist things on our own, staying in very simple places and having a great time.

From there it was off to Munich to study music and art history. That was 1963. Kennedy was dead and memories of the Holocaust were still very much alive. I had an aunt in Munich, as well as family friends. It makes a huge difference in how you get along when you speak the language and can live as ordinary people live. The other students were less involved with war issues than their elders and I went on several trips with them. I had an old decrepit bicycle, figuring it was so old and ugly that no one would want to steal it. I was correct. It did get me around. I had an apartment along the English Gardens where a friend from the U.S. lived with her German husband and their wonderful dog. Her husband was much older than she and told stories of how he hid Jews in his apartment and helped them to get out of Germany. There were many such people who risked a great deal to do what was right.

I met a reporter for the *New York Times* who was doing a survey to determine popular views in Munich at this time. I helped him with his German. The result of the survey was that 75% felt that the Jews got just what they deserved. WOW! A family friend, a psychoanalyst, told me that that belief was the only way they would be able to face themselves. Probably true.

While in Germany I had some opportunities to go to East Berlin with a West German to visit friends of his there. The family had just missed the opportunity to cross over to the West. I remember bringing some fashion magazines for the wife. At the border I was asked why I had so many magazines. I said that I was told I had to wait so long that I decided to bring something to read. It worked. I was deeply impressed at the seriousness of their situation in East Berlin and how sad it was. Yet they had an apartment and lived quite well. They had enough to eat and enough space. What they told me was that they didn't have small freedoms (*kleine freiheiten*) to go and come as they pleased.

During my five or six month stay I made some wonderful friends, had some very long train rides, saw many interesting churches, hospitals, and museums, and enjoyed the culture. I had in depth conversations with many people concerning their history and the complicated politics and culture of the time.

On subsequent trips to Germany I met my mother in Berlin. I have fond memories of walking with her along the Kurfursten Dam and drinking Berliner

Weissere mit Schuss. It is a white beer with a shot of raspberry juice. There is still a web page for this beer, but I'm afraid I still don't like beer.

I was then on my way to England where I rented a room in a house in Wembley, outside of London. There was no central heating and, when I got dressed to go to bed, I put butter on top of the radio so it would melt enough to spread on bread in the morning. It was a short underground ride to London so I could go often. I took a bus to the hospital where I worked, Harefield, which is famous for its lung and heart surgery. We taught breathing and coughing control, as well as related skills involving rehabilitation and some activities of daily living. These skills proved to be very valuable when I returned to work in New York. This type of therapy was helpful in the management of children with cystic fibrosis. At that time the medications were not as sophisticated as they are now, so keeping the lungs clear was a more mechanical process. The therapist in charge, E. Winifred Thacker, wrote the book on the subject. She was so well-known that therapists came from several other countries to learn from her. The hospital was a mini-United Nations which was great fun.

I took the chance to hitchhike through Scotland with a Swedish friend and colleague and then visit Sweden and stay with her family. My uncle knew a Member of Parliament so I was able to visit there, hear him give a speech in the House of Commons, and eat in the dining room nearby Harold Wilson who was Prime Minister at the time.

I found my work in England interesting and I learned a lot. We did work long hours and I gained a valuable insight to the variety of cultures and an introduction to socialized medicine. On the whole, it was very enlightening. The people I was in contact with during my work gave, and received, excellent care. Things were generally somewhat primitive, *i.e.* little central heating and lots of hot water bottles in use.

Did I mention the weather? For the most part it was awful! In all the time I spent overseas, good weather was one month in Spain, one month in Italy, one month in Greece, and one month in England. And the food? I was on a very limited budget so with few exceptions it was forgettable.

In all I spent about a year and a half in 1962-3 with school, travel, and work.

Later, around 1967, I had the opportunity to work in Cape Town, South Africa at the large hospital Groote Schuur. I had some connections and a family friend had some money which she was not permitted to take out. I was the first American physical therapist to work in South Africa. There was static from some friends and family about this venture of mine. There were a few who thought I was either racist or nuts. For me, it was an opportunity. I had just completed a job so off I was again on a ship–this time the *United States*—to the U.K. and on to South Africa.

Once there, I had a lovely room, not far from Table Mountain, and a short bus ride to work. Apartheid was still the way things were in South Africa. It was a much divided country. There were the whites, many tribes of blacks, and the "coloureds"— all separate, very separate. Groote Schuur Hospital is a large general hospital serving all groups. We went from one ward to another; the races being separate but the care, for the most part, equal. The work was both varied and general and I continued to learn. I was fortunate enough to work the weekend of the very first heart transplant done by Dr. Christian Barnard. The patient, whom he had decided did not need chest physical therapy, died in a few days from a related pneumonia. The next heart recipient did receive therapy and lived somewhat longer. As we knew, this surgery was very much in its infancy.

Life in South Africa was in some ways enjoyable. The food was good and mostly prepared by hired help. There was a lot to do and interesting and fun people to do it with, but the fear in the country was pervasive. The people with whom I was in contact were afraid of the blacks, communists, coloreds, and whoever else might be hiding somewhere. There were, of course, exceptions. I had many conversations about everything that was going on. The favorite topic was that things weren't perfect in the States either. However, as I reminded them, we do have laws. Quite a few doctors had left South Africa for the U.S. and elsewhere. For the most part they left because of apartheid. There are many aspects of this social phenomenon that were not always obvious. For example, the concept of teamwork was almost non-existent. In the U.S., hospitals have team meetings which are as effective as the personalities attending them. There a group of patients are discussed by a team. In South Africa, even the idea of a team was foreign. The problem was that, when apartheid was so rigid, many aspects of life were like that, too. I think this deeply affected me. In general, with the pervasive fear and the separate packages, there was for me a lack of depth.

Living in South Africa was difficult for me, however interesting.

Sometimes the best way to find yourself is to travel around the world the way I did, work the way different people work, and live as they do. It isn't easy, but it is enriching.

Summers on the Family Farm

Richard Roof

My home was in Kalamazoo, Michigan and that's where I was born and lived through high school. My father, a dentist, worked there during the cold winter and, as soon as school was out, we moved to the nearby family farm in Coimax. This was a village with about 500 occupants. We had a summer cottage there that was built by my grandfather using lumber from a torn down school house. It was located on Long Lake, a swimming, boating, fishing, place for my brother and me, as well as for our cousins who lived in an adjacent cottage. We spent hours swimming, boating, and exploring that lake and its adjoining marshes, looking for fish, birds, snails, and clams. To add to our collections, we used nets to catch dragonflies and many kinds of butterflies.

Long Lake had an enormous number of snails and clams which had decomposed over millions of years into a grey mud that filled the bottom of the lake. The locals called it *marl* and hauled it away to use as fertilizer on the adjacent farms. We discovered that we could catch clams buried in the marl by pulling up one of the reeds which grew plentifully around the lake and inserting it into the clam's open shell. The clam then closed its shell, gripping what we had inserted. By carefully pulling the reed up we dislodged the clam from the marl and lifted it into our boat. One time we gave some clams to our mother to cook but, unlike sea clams, our freshwater ones tasted terrible.

Our parents had friends who had a cottage on another lake, one called Gun Lake. While visiting there, my brother and I could swim in that body of water. In the bottom of Gun Lake we found a kind of snail that we had never seen before. It was conical in shape and about an inch long with black and yellow stripes around its body. We put some in a jar and took them home to put in our lake. Next year we looked for them and found a few more than we had put there. The year after they were as plentiful as our own kind of snail. Soon those snails had spread throughout the whole lake. We two boys were not aware of the presently known danger of introducing non-native species into another location. However, we never noticed any bad effects of that new snail species.

Like many lakes in Michigan, Long Lake was spring- and rain-filled. It connected to another body of water called Portage Lake where, at its end, the surplus water flowed down a creek. Beavers built a dam across the creek which caused the water level to rise, making it easier for them to cut down trees. This controlled the water level in both lakes. Of course, for swimming, we boys liked the water high. Then one day we found the lake level getting lower. We canoed over to the beaver dam on Portage Lake to see why the water level was going down. What we discovered was that the dam had been torn apart and water was rushing down the creek. The previous water level had gotten so high that it had not only flooded the trees for the beavers' benefit; it had also flooded the pasture on an adjacent farm. The farmer, named Dyer, had made a hole in the dam to stop the flooding of his pasture. We kids tried to patch the dam but, in a night or two, the beavers did a much better job of it. (For years we called that man "old man Dyer.")

Sixty years later, when we moved to the Saratoga Retirement Community, I met a resident who said that he was from Michigan. When I asked him whereabouts in the state, he said, "Coimax, Michigan." I had never before met anyone who had come from that town! Then I learned that his name was Dyer, Jim Dyer, and that his father owned a farm that backed up on Portage Lake. His father was "old man Dyer!" While I was enjoying the summer at the lake, he was helping his father on that farm and attending Coimax High School in the winter. Not only that, he dated two of my older cousins, Peggy and Martie.

The next time I was in Climax I visited Peggy and told her that I had met him. She remembered Jim Dyer very well. Afterwards I took a photo of her and her husband and gave it to him. We both enjoyed reminiscing about the lumber company, the post office, and Sinclair's grocery which is still there. That post office was the very first in the United States to deliver mail to farmers using RFD—Rural Free Delivery.

Peggy lived on my Uncle Fred's farm. In high school she was what today we call a server in the first drive-in ice cream shop in Michigan. Those were the days when ice cream was still made with the heavy cream that came with it naturally. Uncle Fred operated the village dairy. He milked his cows, separated the cream, and made ice cream in the back of his farmhouse. A driveway circled the house and we drove to the back in our family's 1936 Chrysler. That's where Peggy appeared to take our ice cream order and bring it to the car. In addition to the town dairy, Uncle Fred was the only local person who had a welding machine. At harvest time in the summer all the farmers came to his place to have their harvesting equipment repaired. I remember seeing a long line of harvesting machines drawn by horses and tractors lined up waiting to be repaired.

Another first occurred on my grandfather's farm when the first harvesting combine was demonstrated there in 1836. Hiram Moore and John Hascall's harvesting machine was drawn about on a field of wheat that was ready to be harvested. It cut the wheat, and threshed it, separating the wheat grain from the straw—that is, the wheat stalks. The wheat grains were collected in a bin and the straw was blown back on the ground where it could later be raked up for use as livestock bedding and fodder. That machine is believed to be the forerunner of the modern combine and the more celebrated McCormick Reaper, the harvester that could cut and thresh up to 20 acres a day. However, that first model was so huge that it took a team of 16 horses to pull it. Eventually it proved impractical in its original application. A stone monument with a brass plate describing the first demonstration stands on the farm today.

Our family farm produced apple and peach trees in an orchard that required considerable work in the summer. The trees needed to be sprayed every week to get rid of fungus and insects. When it was ready, the fruit was hand-picked and sorted for sale. Some of it was sold to nearby grocery stores for two dollars a bushel. Later we adopted a "you-pick" plan allowing people to pick the fruit for themselves.

An essential part of growing apples and peaches was to have sufficient bees to pollinate the trees in the spring. We maintained an apiary which my uncle had set up for that purpose, one that consisted of 15-20 colonies of bees whose honey we ourselves ate or sold. That uncle was the one who taught me the basics of bee-keeping.

As the bees filled their combs with honey it was necessary to add empty combs for the incoming honey. These combs came in boxes called "supers" and, as they were added, the hive got higher and higher. Before opening a bee hive, beekeepers use a smoker to blow smoke into the hive entrance to calm the bees. I learned how to use one—a can of burning wood with a bellows attached. Smokers are also used while examining the combs whenever the bees become agitated.

To maintain honey production, the frames of the bee combs had to be examined every week to look for, and destroy, any enlarged cells in them that contained bee larva destined to become queen bees. If those were allowed to reach maturity and a queen was hatched, most of the bees and the old queen would fly away to start a new home. This process was called "swarming." The new queen and a reduced force of worker—that is, honey collecting—bees were all that was left in the original colony. Without that weekly inspection, honey production from that colony would be reduced.

As I became more interested in beekeeping, my father helped me start additional bee colonies. We ordered bees from the Sears Roebuck catalog. They arrived by parcel post in screened cages and with enough food to last a week. They were dumped into a new beehive with combs which I had assembled from components also bought from the Sears Roebuck catalog.

At 13, when I was in junior high school, I was old enough to take charge of the apiary for the orchard. The job of taking care of the bees fell to me and my reward was to be able to sell the honey the bees produced. At that time, during World War II, sugar was rationed so people eagerly bought honey to supplement their meager sugar ration. I also sold the honey to local grocery stores for 34 cents for an eight-ounce bottle. I used the money to buy new equipment. I bought a centrifuge to extract the honey from the combs. It had a valve at the bottom to allow the honey to fill each of the bottles. One day I forgot to close the valve tightly. When I returned to use it again, thousands of bees were swarming around to collect the honey which had run out all over the floor. I fled in alarm. Later my mother helped me clean up the spilled honey.

We had a lot of sugar maple trees on our property and my father taught me how to "tap" them so we could make maple syrup. The process involved cutting a six-inch piece of the stem of the plentiful Michigan sumac trees. The bark of the stem was whittled off and its pith was pushed out, making it a wooden tube. Then one or more holes were drilled in a maple tree and a wooden tube was pounded in each hole.

For drilling holes I used my father's brace and bit, an old tool dating from Pilgrim days, to make a hole in the maple tree out in our front yard. I cut a branch from a sumac tree in the nearby woods and removed the pith. After pounding the stick into the tree, the sap almost instantly began dripping out. I had hung a pail on the stick and sap began to fill the pail. After I collected the sap every night and morning for a week, there was enough for my mother to begin boiling it to make it concentrate. She produced about a half cup of maple syrup, boiling it for a day on a gas range. My elementary school, Hillcrest School, learned about my maple syrup project and I showed my sixth grade class how to tap maple trees. I remember that we tapped the row of maple trees alongside the school playground, but I don't recall what happened to the sap.

All in all, my farm experiences were an education that city boys don't get.

A Weatherman's World

I wanted to fly, but my interest changed…

Jim Kistler

As a youngster I grew up in Lawrence, Kansas where my Dad taught journalism at the University of Kansas. It was in the Depression years when my mother and father, brother and sister, grandmother and aunt, and I all lived in a small house with a large dog and two cats. We lived not far from the Haskel Indian Reservation and often went there to see tribal demonstrations and military shows. This was also the time when Spain was fighting a civil war and Germany and Italy were helping Franco's forces. It was of interest to me as my Dad had fought in World War I and was still active in the Kansas National Guard. Military aviation intrigued me and my Dad introduced me to several pilot friends who had stayed on active duty.

Years passed but my love for aviation remained and in the early 1940s I knew I wanted to fly in the military. During the World War II years I was in high school. My brother, two years older than me, joined the Navy in 1944, but I remained in high school until the war ended in 1945. When I graduated in 1946, I was determined to fly, but by that time my eyesight had deteriorated so much that I knew I would have to go to college and follow another career. I worked summers and after school, accumulating sufficient money and set it aside to go to the University of Michigan partly on scholarships. My brother returned from the Navy and, in 1946, we both went to the U. of M., he to the Engineering School and me to the Business School. After two semesters of economics and science courses in geology, I decided

I liked geological science the most. I soon was taking more physics, chemistry, mathematics, and geology. After mostly technical courses during the remaining two and one-half years, plus summer geological field camp in the Teton Range of Wyoming, I graduated with a B. S. degree in June of 1950.

Prior to my graduation I had applied for, and had been accepted for, a Teaching Assistant post at Northwestern University for the following two years. I was pretty sure my career path was already settled. I had also been given a summer field geology training assignment with the U. S. Geological Survey, which fit in well, so I was off first to Denver and then to work near Fort Peck, Montana. No sooner had I arrived than North Korea invaded South Korea and the U. S. was involved again. In mid-August I got a draft notice from my Draft Board back in my home in Michigan, telling me to report for a pre-induction physical exam the next day. Obviously, that wouldn't work. So, after a few phone calls, my local Board arranged for me to transfer my physical to Glasgow, Montana, where I subsequently joined another group of potential inductees. We shortly entrained across the mountains for Butte, Montana where we were given our physical exams. I passed and was told my records would be sent back to my original Draft Board in Michigan. Fortunately for me, I returned home before my draft records arrived. At that time if you were enrolled in college before you received your induction orders you could remain in college.

I lucked out and was able to enroll at Northwestern, begin my graduate teaching and study, and thus was allowed to continue my work until I finished Graduate School some two years later. In the interim I was offered, and accepted, a geological position with the Standard Oil Company of California. Some two months later I saw that the Air Force was recruiting college graduates with math, physics, chemistry, and geology degrees for training in Advanced Meteorology at various universities. As a potential backup, should I not be given a deferment, I applied for this program, as well. I graduated from Northwestern in mid-June and the same day heard from the Draft Board that my deferment had been denied, and I was to be inducted into the Army on July 1, 1952.

That left only the Air Force. After several calls, I was advised that I had been accepted into their program, that they were waiting for Graduate School acceptance. I then called headquarters, Air Weather Service, in Washington, D. C., talked to a Colonel who said he'd take care of it. The next morning my Draft Board informed me that I was deferred until I was sworn into the Air Force. Thus began my Air Force career…

I left home in late August, flying on my first commercial DC-3 aircraft, to Indianapolis where I joined a group of other weather-forecasting candidates at an induction base. After several weeks of physical exams, dental work, uniform-fitting, and more, we were sent to St. Louis University for graduate degree training in Meteorology. Our instructors were all professors working for the Air Force, teaching a bunch of math and physics and other science majors how to forecast for military aviation. After a full year of instruction, we graduated as weather forecasters. Thereafter 32 of the original 38 were shipped to San Antonio, Texas, to Lackland Air Force base, (the "Gateway to the Air Force.") After two plus months at OBMC (Officers Basic Military Course), which included small arms, marching, and other military courses, we graduated and were commissioned Second Lieutenants.

We got our orders in October and, since the Korean conflict was still active, many of the group headed to California for shipment to Korea. Three of us drove together to Parks Air Force Station outside San Francisco. The next day my orders were changed and I was sent to Hamilton Air Force Base, California outside San Rafael. This was a fighter interceptor base at the time responsible for west coast air defense. While there, I learned a lot of weather-related functions from work in the "block house" which had no windows, for secrecy reasons. As the winter progressed, the weather challenges became more demanding. There wasn't much in the way of weather radar support in those days. Aerial weather reconnaissance was utilized a lot to obtain surface and upper air data. World War II had demonstrated the need to get information about upper air winds, temperature gradient, storm tracks, location and strength of newly recognized jet stream data, and more. Upper air data from balloons were fairly common, but precise information over large water bodies, such as the Pacific, was more difficult. The information we collected was utilized in making forecast maps over the major oceans.

I was selected for training for flights on the west coast from Sacramento into the Gulf of Alaska and back: 16 hour flights in converted weather WB50 aircraft (similar to B-29s of World War II). They were strenuous flights! Before I had made many of these training flights, I received another change in orders and was advised that I was being transferred to the European Theater of operations. Shortly thereafter I was on my way from Hamilton to Tripoli, Libya. Unfortunately, my aspirations to fly weather reconnaissance were blocked, but other challenges awaited me.

Once I arrived in Tripoli I was sent to get a Spanish passport since Spain was to be my new destination. I was assigned to one of the new Strategic Air Command bases opened in eastern Spain. I was elated, but soon I heard that I was reassigned again, and shortly was flying to Athens, Greece to a small Air Force station at the Athens International Airport. My assignment there included not only weather forecasting with JUSMAG (Joint U. S. Military Aid to Greece), but also support for Air Force flights between Germany, Rome, Tripoli, Athens, and NATO stations in Izmir, Ankara, and Adana, Turkey. Later I found I was also responsible for weather support to a "spook" air squadron (a specialized secret squadron) that had missions over the Balkan countries that were aligned with the Soviets during the Cold War. The Korean conflict had ended, but Russian relationships with the U. S. were strained. Many Communists in Greece were actively supporting the Soviet cause. We, on our part, sent upper air balloons over the Balkan countries that dropped propaganda pamphlets, trying to influence those who were not avid Communists. We also supported Hungarians loyal to the pre-conquest government, and others who flew over the homelands at night in unmarked aircraft for the same propaganda purposes.

Shortly after my assignment to Greece, I was quartered in a nice hotel in Athens, not far from the airport. I soon found that other transients were staying there while on route to their destinations. One group was assigned to the daily air evacuation flights that were, among other things, bringing back injured Turkish soldiers returning home from Korea. It turned out that the flight nurses and their crews stayed in my hotel most nights. My forecasting duty ended about 7 p.m. and I ate at the same hotel restaurant. It wasn't long before I had a chance to meet the various nurses there. While I was working at the airport one morning I took a coffee break. An air evacuation jeep pulled up and a pretty nurse in the back seat asked if I wanted a ride. I was only about a half block from my destination, but I hopped into the back seat next to her. That evening while several pilots and I were playing poker, drinking a beer or two, and were somewhat boisterous, the phone rang and a sweet nurse's voice said, "You're making a lot of noise! By the way, what is your blood type?" When I told her "A-neg", she replied, "I'm B-neg, and I've been looking for an A-neg." I found out later that nurses felt these two were a good combination. From then on we got along very well. Not much later her flight nurse squadron in Germany decided to open a small two-nurse station in Athens with three male technicians. My nurse friend, Rita, applied and was put in charge of the small five-person unit. Rita and her nurse friend got a nice apartment with a view of the Aegean Sea, and I ended up with two pilots in a small house overlooking the end of the airport runway.

Over six months we got to be close buddies and her friend, Shirley, told me, "You'd better get serious with a ring!" But I was always a bit slow! One day, after Rita had flown to Germany, where I knew she had another boyfriend, she returned with a big diamond on her left hand. I was devastated and set about convincing her that she was planning to marry the wrong guy. I finally gave her my college fraternity pin, but I didn't think she felt this was a big commitment. Shortly afterwards I flew with her to Tripoli and, at Wheelus Field, got her a large diamond the right size for her finger. On Valentine's Day 1956, her roommate, Shirley, threw a big engagement party for many of our friends on the base. Unfortunately, Shirley got called on an emergency flight to Ankara that day. The weather turned bad, and she couldn't get back for the party.

Rita was sent to the States in February to Clovis Air Force Base in New Mexico, applied for release from active duty in the Air Force and, upon release, headed for her hometown in Indiana. Just before she left Clovis, she had to "stand a retreat" when the base General gave her a commendation medal for her performance in Athens. This is a woman who, six years earlier, when she entered the Air Force from nurses' training, hadn't known much about military protocol—even who to salute and what to wear on her uniform! She liked silver more than gold so bought silver bars rather than the proper gold ones she was supposed to wear as a Second Lieutenant.

I was released from active duty in the Air Force in late August of 1956 in time to join my future wife in Indiana. Since my home was also on Lake Michigan, some 150 miles north of Rita's town, we were married in her home church. Thereafter we had a honeymoon in the Finger Lakes of New York and headed off for California where my long delayed geological job resumed. That's another story, one which includes 23 years of active Reserve duty in the Air Force as part of the 35 years of geological and geophysical work with Chevron in various locations—from Salinas to Bakersfield to Alaska, to San Francisco, to England, and back to San Francisco where I finally retired.

Why I Remain an Alien

John Price

The town straddled the river Leam, which meandered placidly between well-tended parks and gardens, until it flowed out of the town and into the Avon. On the north side of the river Leam were the "Pump Rooms and Baths", built in 1814 to exploit the local mineral springs, and proclaimed to provide "cures for diverse ailments". These resources helped the town become a popular spa resort which grew a hundred-fold in population to nearly 27,000 by the beginning of the 20th century.

Much of the town's building development in the 19th century conformed to an elegant Regency or Neo-Georgian architectural style with classical details and decorative ironwork on many of the houses well preserved to this day. The houses were set on wide streets, tree-lined avenues and open squares, quite unlike the ancient town of Warwick, just two miles to the west. In 1838 Queen Victoria visited the town and was "graciously pleased" to bestow upon it the Royal Warrant, which allowed the town to use "Royal" in its name.

It was to this town, Royal Leamington Spa, that my parents and my older brother Peter came to make our home in 1938 when I was just one year old. The house we lived in had, as I recall, a long back garden, with a lawn and trees nearer to the house and, further back, a vegetable garden which my father loved to tend. He also had a chicken coop which provided us with lots of fresh eggs. For tea, my brother and I would each have bread and butter with a soft-boiled egg sitting in an eggcup. My eggcup had a happy yellow chick painted on it (apparently unaware that I was eating its embryonic siblings). I used a small spoon to crack open the top of the eggshell and dig out the delicious contents. My mother taught us a song which we sang before tea-time:

Say, little hen,
When when when
Will you lay
Me an egg
For my tea?

When my father was drafted into the Army, my mother and I took care of the chickens. I loved to sit in the coop, watch the chickens, and talk to them. One night we heard a hullabaloo coming from the coop and found out the next morning that a fox had got in and killed a chicken. However, it must have been frightened off because it hadn't eaten its victim. My mother and brother dug a hole in the ground to bury the corpse, but neither of them would touch it, so I volunteered. I felt quite important carrying it from the coop and putting it in its tiny grave.

In the front of the house I had my own small bedroom, with a dormer window and diamond-shaped leaded panes. I loved to sit in the dormer and observe the daily activities outside, from the horse-drawn milk cart in the early morning to the gas-lamp lighter at twilight who walked from post to post, lighting them with a long pole that he used to turn on the gas and then ignite it.

Not far across the road was a railway line, the London, Midland and Scottish (LMS), which carried little traffic until the war started in 1939. The Great Western Railway (GWR) also ran through town, and there was a small electrified railway line that ran to Stratford-Upon-Avon. Other forms of transportation included the Midland Red bus company and the Grand Union Canal for freight. I used to enjoy long walks along that canal path, especially where it crossed the river Avon and the Great Western Railway on tall aqueducts.

Behind our house were open fields where cattle and sheep grazed and beyond the fields lay the river Leam. Close to that river were natural springs, which my brother, our friends, and I would occasionally dam and dig canals to channel the water in various directions. The Leam played a large role in my early years. I learned to fish with homemade tackle, built a raft which we paddled with our cricket bats, and even ice-skated during the viciously cold winter of 1948/49. Many birds made the river their home, including stately swans. They were at home in the water but struggled hard to become airborne, mightily flapping their wings for many yards before escaping the pull of the river.

At the top of our street (Princes Drive) was a small railway station, from where trains could be taken north to Kenilworth and Coventry, or southeast to central Leamington. Mounted on the brick wall outside the station were candy machines from which Cadbury's chocolate bars had once been on sale for a few pence. However, by the time I was old enough to become aware of these machines, wartime rationing had made them obsolete, so there they sat, empty and rusting away, but still advertising their wares to hungry little boys. Later, they brought to my mind paintings from the Leamington Art Gallery in which peasants wandered through the Italian countryside with the ruins of Roman temples about them; the temples represented the glories of a past civilization, just as the candy machines represented a pre-war civilization that I had never experienced.

When I was almost four, Germany launched an aerial attack that was the most severe to hit Coventry during the war. The city was barely eight miles north of Leamington, and my father still worked there until he joined up. He had constructed a steel prefabricated shelter in our family room and equipped it with bunks. When the sirens sounded at night, my parents carried Peter and me downstairs to our bunks in the shelter. Not understanding the danger, I loved the thrill of these occasions with the wail of the sirens, the roar of the planes overhead, and the rare thud of a wayward bomb!

That massive raid (Operation Moonlight Sonata) was designed to destroy Coventry's industrial base, although damage to the rest of the city was considerable. Wave after wave of bombers dropped high explosive and incendiary bombs throughout the night. Some bombs even fell on Leamington, too. The final all-clear was sounded at 6:15 the following morning. My father took the train to Coventry as far as it could go, then walked the remaining miles. However, he could not find his workplace or even the street; all was flattened, including nearby Coventry Cathedral. Over 400 homes were destroyed and almost 500 people lost their lives.

In 1945 the war ended. I was eight and by then avidly reading everything I could find. The newspapers wrote mostly about the wars in Europe and the Pacific, and very little else. In my mind, they existed primarily to report war news. Consequently I was quite astonished to discover that newspapers did not cease publication after the war, but still managed to find plenty to write about. To older people it must have seemed like a return to the old ways of life; to me, it was a bewildering transition into a brave new world!

At the age of eleven, I won a scholarship to Warwick, an independent boys' school founded in 914 *a.d.* and believed to be the oldest extant boys' school in the world. Although it had boarding facilities, I lived close enough to be able to bicycle there six days a week (Monday through Friday and Saturday morning). Other boys came by bus from Coventry, Kenilworth, and other outlying towns. I remember one lucky fellow who lived on a farm and rode his horse to school every day!

During my second year at Warwick, the Headmaster, who was trying to revive a classics tradition, persuaded me and three other boys to take Latin and Greek, with little time left over for science. After three years of the classics, I was informed that I would also have to give up mathematics to specialize solely in ancient languages and history. At this point, I rebelled and said I would no longer take classics, as mathematics had always been my favorite subject. Luckily, an understanding teacher came to my rescue. He suggested that I concentrate on mathematics and physics. He also provided me with several physics books to read during the summer holidays. Without his support I might never have pursued a career in physics.

Another turning point in my life occurred that summer. One of my classics friends had an aunt living in Paris who offered him and three of his friends the use of her apartment for two weeks. He asked two other boys and me if we would like to go. Of course we said, "Yes!" but then we had to persuade our parents to help us with all the travel expenses. A big meeting was held with the four of us and all our parents and it was finally agreed that we could go.

We had all taken French for several years, but I don't believe any one of us had actually tried it out on an actual French person. Had our French teachers done a good job? That was the time to find out. We flew from Heathrow to Orly airport on *British European Airways*, and transferred to a bus to take us to the city. For some unknown reason, the driver was in a hurry and, every time he cornered, we slid around on the bench seats. "This isn't safe," said an American girl who was sitting next to me. "I'll fall off the seat unless you hold onto me." Appreciating the impeccable logic of her request, I put my arm around her shoulders. My heart murmured to me, *"La vie est belle."* I was already thinking in French!

The apartment was excellent, a short walk from the Bastille metro station, but long enough to encounter neighborhood cafés and patisseries. The Bastille prison itself was no more, having been destroyed during the French revolution. For two weeks, the four of us walked all over Paris, absorbing all we could of French culture, past and present. There was so much to see and learn (and smell!). As we walked the streets, my nose kept telling me something was different—ah, garlic!

One night, we bought the cheapest seats to the Paris opera and went to see the opera *Rigoletto*. Our seats were high up in the rear of the theatre: the program and synopsis of the opera were in French, as was the singing, and most of the scenes were set in semi-darkness! Nevertheless, despite failing to comprehend most of the plot, I was completely overwhelmed by the music; the individual arias, duets, and the quartet *"Bella figlia dell'amore"* had a beauty of their own unlike that of orchestral music. For me it was an epiphany, a revealing vision of opera that I had failed to appreciate before that performance.

Finally it was time to leave Paris, but as usual we were late and barely managed to catch the airport bus, which was waiting for us. As we boarded, a man in a pilot's uniform said to us, "Come on, lads, you're going to miss your flight." We apologized and sat down alongside him. He then asked us what flight we were taking from Orly. When we told him, he said, "Well, you're in luck, lads, I'm your pilot."

Returning to life at Warwick School, with help from my teachers and fellow students, I was able to catch up with the physics curriculum before long. I began to appreciate its power to change our lives, just as I had felt about mathematics a few years earlier. I remember on one occasion, when learning differential calculus, I experienced a wild feeling of power, and thought to myself, *"With this knowledge, I could rule the world!"*

Later on, in my final year at Warwick, my career advisor gave me a small book about the role of physicists in our lives. I still remember a definition from the book: *"A physicist is a believer in the material origin of vital phenomena."* I thought to myself that this was exactly how I felt. There was no need to invoke religion, miracles, or dogma in attempting to explain the real world. The scientific method worked so much better. Also in the book was a controversial quotation attributed to Ernest Rutherford, a famous physicist from New Zealand, who said: *"The only real science is physics, all the rest is just stamp collecting."*

After leaving Warwick School, I went to Nottingham University. Living in a large town like Nottingham gave me the opportunity to experience the performing arts more fully, seeing live theatre, symphony, and opera. Also, there was a thriving nightlife, with steel drum and skiffle bands playing in the pubs and coffee bars. (Skiffle music originated in the American South but underwent a revival in England in the 1950s. The instruments used included washboards, tea chest bass, and guitars). It was a wonderful time to be young, and free to experience what life had to offer. After three years at Nottingham, I received a degree in physics and electronics. Just over a year later, I had left England behind to begin a new life in America.

I left England on April 20, 1960, boarding the SS *United States* that was to take me from Southampton to New York. My parents had driven me down from Leamington Spa, staying overnight in Salisbury where we found time to visit the magnificent cathedral. We said "Goodbye" on the docks in Southampton, all of us crying. I felt terrible, as if I had let them down by leaving. We hugged and I climbed aboard the ship. I still regret that I never truly thanked them for all they had done for me, then or later.

Sailing on the SS *United States* was a wonderful experience and I am glad that I chose to sail rather than fly to the USA. At that time it was the fastest cruise ship in the world, making the crossing in under five days. On April 25 we reached New York. It was early morning, foggy, and there was a gasp from all on deck as the fog lifted to reveal the inspiring Statue of Liberty.

I spent two days exploring the city before flying to Pittsburgh to be met by my new manager, Bill Hugle, whom I had never seen before. In London I had been interviewed by another person several months earlier and had been offered a position at Westinghouse's new semiconductor research lab. Driving to the lab from the airport, Bill quickly discovered that I had little or no knowledge of integrated circuits and logic design which was his department's mission. So upon arriving at the lab, he gave me a bunch of textbooks to read, saying: "Here, when you've read these, come and talk to me."

Rather than spending all my time reading the books, I decided to walk around the lab and find out what everybody was doing. Coming from England, it was for me quite a culture shock. I met people from all over the US, Canada, Germany, France, Italy, Spain, and even Syria. Although they all spoke English, some had odd accents and idioms and unpronounceable last names. But they went out of their way to be friendly and helpful and soon they had found me a place to stay and rides to work.

After about a week enduring the hot, humid weather of Pittsburgh in spring, I decided that I had to find some lightweight clothing to replace the thick wool suits that I brought with me from England. On Saturday my new friends took me to Kaufman's department store in Pittsburgh and we descended to the bargain basement. I found a lightweight jacket that fitted me, and the salesman congratulated me on my choice. "How would you like to pay for this, John?" he said. (He had already found out my first name.) "Will that be cash or charge?"

Well, "cash" I understood, but what was meant by "charge"? He explained how simple it was to open a charge account and pay so much a month for my purchases. "That sounds very nice," I said. He directed me to a room on the fifth floor which was filled with cubicles, each with a table and two chairs, and signs around the walls which proclaimed in large red letters: CREDIT: ONE MAN'S FAITH IN ANOTHER.

I sat down and was soon greeted warmly by a gentleman to whom I explained my desire to open a charge account. "Yes," he said, "it's very easy. All we do is ask you three simple questions." This is getting better and better, I thought, surely these questions can't be too hard?

His first question was "How long have been living in this area?" "One week." I responded. I thought his smile changed a little. "Second question: How long have you been working?" "One week," I responded again. By now, I sensed that things were not going too well! "We have one more question: Do you have a checking account with a bank?" "No," I said, "I'm afraid I don't." I knew I was doomed!

"Mr. Price," he said, "You failed all three questions, and consequently, we will not be able to open a charge account." Quickly grasping at straws, I pointed to the red signs on the walls, and said: "What about 'CREDIT, ONE MAN'S FAITH IN ANOTHER'?" "I didn't write the signs," he said. "I'm afraid we can't help you." At this point I returned to the basement and paid cash for my jacket. Many years were to pass before I ever acquired a credit card.

My next adventure with American retail establishments occurred when I realized that I needed a car to get around, even though I lived only a short walking distance from work. Again my friends drove me, this time to a used car lot. When the salesman asked me what car I was interested in, I felt quite confident in my response, as I had read a library book about American cars prior to leaving England. "Well," I said, "My first choice is a Cord." The salesman responded that Cords had ceased production in 1937. (I was unaware how out of date my library book had been.) "OK, my second choice is a Hudson." The salesman, obviously an expert in his knowledge of extinct automobiles, explained that Hudsons had not been made since 1957 and there were none on the lot. Now I was down to my last choice. "Do you have any Studebakers?" I asked. "Well," he said, "the company is on its last legs but I do have a beautiful 1956 Studebaker Hawk." It certainly was beautiful and I bought it for $600. It was the second car I had ever owned and later on I drove it all the way to California.

After 15 months in Pennsylvania, I was offered a position at Fairchild Semiconductor Research Labs in Palo Alto, California. This was a plum opportunity as Fairchild was the leader in integrated circuit development, so I wasted no time in accepting their offer. As I was to find out after living in Silicon Valley for a while, the political culture was so different from my first experiences in America. Back east the prevalent feeling seemed to be "You can't beat City Hall", coupled with a fervent anti-Communist paranoia. Conversely, on the west coast, I was energized by a "We can change it. Anything is possible" feeling of enthusiasm!

In "Auguries of Innocence" William Blake wrote:

To see a world in a grain of sand
And a heaven in a wild flower.
Hold infinity in the palm of your hand
And eternity in an hour.

To me, these words beautifully described integrated circuit technology. A "grain of sand" was a silicon chip containing millions of transistors and interconnections, almost "infinity in the palm of your hand." A transistor could switch on and off many trillions of times in an hour, whereas turning a light switch on and off once a second would take thirty thousand years (an "eternity") to achieve what the transistor accomplished in a single hour.

When I arrived in Silicon Valley, integrated circuit development was still in its infancy and consequently the pace of technological growth was feverish. The products that we were creating were pervasive, affecting people's lives in a multitude of ways. However, in the early 60s I was not aware of the future impact that our products would have upon society. I think that Nevil Chute, in *A Town Like Alice* expressed my feelings perfectly when he wrote: "It seems to me that I have been mixed up in things far greater than I realized at the time."

The 60s also saw major changes in my personal life. I married Rosalie, a San Francisco native (now my wife of 50 years), had a son, and learned the challenging new responsibilities of being a parent and a concerned member of society. We became involved participants in protests against the Vietnam War and marching as a family with our young son, Michael, on my back.

For many years, I lived in America as a lawful resident alien, but in 1984 I decided to apply for naturalization. However, I took exception to Question 18 of the application, which said:

"List your present and past membership in or affiliation
with every organization, association, fund, foundation,
party, club, society or similar group in the United States
or in any other country or place."

I refused to answer this question, on the basis that the question was overly broad and impinged upon my rights of free association protected by the First Amendment. Moreover, I had already answered in the negative all questions concerning affiliation with Communist or totalitarian organizations.

With the help of lawyers working *pro bono* for the ACLU and after waiting three years for a response from the Immigration and Naturalization Service (INS), a hearing was set to appear before the US District Court for Northern California. Unfortunately the court entered a judgment in favor of the INS.

In 1989 we filed an appeal to the Ninth Circuit of the US Court of Appeals, but in 1991 the three-judge panel in a split vote ruled to uphold the decision of the District Court, stating that First Amendment issues could not be invoked in the context of naturalization. In other words, I was guaranteed First Amendment rights as a resident alien or as a citizen, but not during the act of applying for naturalization!.

The dissenting judge, John Noonan wrote as follows:

"The Immigration Service propounds a question to persons seeking naturalization that would be intolerable if asked by a government agency of an American citizen. It chills the right of free association guaranteed by the First Amendment.

The Immigration Service's answer is that aliens are different. They are second-class people. No doubt for some purposes this characterization is the harsh truth. Since the abolition of slavery, aliens are the only adults subject to treatment as second-class people in the United States.

The alien is a resident of long standing—in the present case 30 years. Realistically such a person has been conducting himself like an American for a very long time.

His reactions to an intolerable inquiry are similar to those of a citizen. Rightly so. He has imbibed the air of freedom which permeates our culture. He insists upon a right not to be treated as a second-class person where freedom of association is concerned.

Mr. Price lawfully entered this country and resides here. He is invested with the rights guaranteed by the Constitution to all people within our borders."

At this point the ACLU lawyers could have reasonably considered the case closed, but instead they went on to petition the US Supreme Court. Unfortunately, the Supreme Court chose not to hear the appeal. Even then, all was not over. I met Congressman Tom Campbell, who agreed that the INS was treating applicants for naturalization in a constitutionally impermissible manner. He began preparing legislation to change this, but his term of office came to an end in 2001, prior to any such legislation being enacted.

Over twenty years have passed since Judge Noonan wrote his inspiring opinion. I am older now, possibly wiser, but sadly still an alien.

Summarizing a Life

Don Schmidek (with Jan Schmidek)

Some years ago, in the former Yugoslavia, in the town of Zagreb, I was born into a loving and large family. My mother came from a long lineage of merchants, lawyers, land and forest owners, lumber business owners, architects and politicians. They had settled in Zagreb a few centuries before, when the country was part of the Austro-Hungarian Empire. Her great-grandfather fathered nine children in the early 1800's, who in turn were very productive. One of the daughters had five children. Her grandfather had four children, one of which was her mother. Her mother had three children, one was my mother, who finally was sensible and had just two children: one boy and one girl. That boy was me.

On my father's side, my grandfather was born in 1857 and my father in 1905, in the small town of Nova Gradiška. This was a river town, part of the Austro-Hungarian Empire border zone. It was strategically positioned as the seat of the regional government. The family was in the wholesale and commerce business, with shipping transports up and down the Sava-Danube Rivers. Sometime in the 1920s, after the establishment of Yugoslavia, my grandfather retired, moved the family to Zagreb, Croatia, and sent my father to France to study Engineering.

In Paris my father met my mother's brother, and through him, my mother, who at that time was studying in Switzerland. To make a long story short, they met, fell in love, and married after graduating from their respective universities.

My parents' wedding presents were substantial. They received a couple of apartments houses (her architect father designed and built these) and a factory (financed by his father)! In a short time my father was the largest independent producer of light bulbs in Yugoslavia, one with sufficient output to brighten many homes, streets, trams, trains, and even businesses and government locals. An interesting sideline is that the name of the factory was "DIS" which stood for "Domaca Industria Sijalica" or "Domestic Industry of Light Bulbs", but also represents the first initials of my names!!

Life in the 1930s was comfortable and prosperous. We had a very large family that met on almost a weekly basis at various residences, villas, or other places. In the summers we went to the Adriatic Sea for several weeks and in the winters to the Yugoslav Alps, to ski.

In 1941 the war broke out. The Germans and Italians invaded Yugoslavia which capitulated in eight days. They brought with them several "puppet" fascist governments and Yugoslavia was split into several nations. Then began the persecutions of the old kingdom's government supporters and politicians—Romas, Serbs (in Croatia), Orthodox Christians, Muslims, and Jews. During the 1941-1945 period, out of the previous 14 million Yugoslav inhabitants, over 1 million were exterminated in various local and German slave camps.

Due to my family's association with the previous "kingdom's" government all our properties were confiscated. My mother's wisdom and foresight made us request and obtain (with the passage of money) permission to travel to Italy. Once the four of us (father, mother, sister and myself) were on the train close to the Italian border, for unclear reasons, we were thrown off it by the Italians. We were lucky that we were near to the town where we used to spend our summer vacations. One of our old friends owned a villa on the Adriatic waterfront which he opened to us. This section of Croatia was under Italian control, where old political affiliation and racial profiling were very low on the local Italian military government's priority. Eventually, due to some negotiations between higher ups in the Italian, German, and Croatian governments, we were interned in two Italian Civilian Internment Camps in Croatia, together with Slovene Partisan prisoners. Life was not easy, but there was no forced labor or gas chambers, which prevailed in the German and Croatian camps. We were able to keep our possessions (jewels, gold, and money) which served us well in obtaining better treatment and more food from the gentler (!) Italian officers and soldiers.

In September of 1943 Italy capitulated to the Allies and we were free to leave the camp. Back to Croatian mainland we went and followed Tito's partisans for several months, while being chased and bombed by the German Armies.

Two interesting and memorable episodes occurred around January of 1944 in the town of Senj. This is a little coastal town of Croatia with a small harbor and a centuries-old fort on the hill above the town. For some strange reason the leader of the Jugoslav Partisans, Tito, decided to have his "fleet" come to the town's harbor for a celebration. That celebration culminated with the Germans dropping leaflets on the town in the morning and later in the afternoon dropping bombs on us and sinking the fleet. As those bombs started falling, the church priest grabbed all of us children and whisked us into the crypt below the church altar. After the planes left, when we climbed back into the church, we noticed a hole in the church ceiling and a 125 Kg bomb lying in front of the altar. As we left the church, we saw another, similar, bomb on the front steps. Neither one had exploded! If either one had, we could have been trapped in the crypt.

A few days later I went with my uncle to a munitions warehouse that the Italians had left still full of various artillery shells, bags of dynamite, assorted munitions and some flares. I reached for one of the flares and pulled the string… The flare went screeching toward the high ceiling and came gently down by parachute, brightly burning. Luckily it landed on the bare floor and not on a bag of dynamite! Had it landed there, I think I would not be here writing this. Suffice it to say, my uncle was not very pleased with me!

Eventually we left the town of Senj by boarding small boats and arrived 14 days later at Vis, an island in the Adriatic that had been occupied recently by the British. After some weeks there, we were transported to a British holding camp in Bari, Italy and told that our next stop would be Africa.

By some coincidence, my mother's father and brother, who previously had managed to get to Italy ahead of us, in 1942, on a train that had departed earlier than ours, were living in the town of Taranto, not far from Bari. A bribe persuaded an Italian truck driver to drive us there out of our British "resort." The British guards couldn't have cared less when we packed up and left, right through the main gate.

Our reunion with grandfather and uncle was joyous. We obtained a furnished apartment in Taranto, which had been vacated by owners who were Fascist sympathizers, and who had fled north when the Allies invaded Italy. We were fortunate since my father obtained a position with the British Army, due to his language and technical abilities, and thus we qualified for British weekly food rations of meat, margarine, and chips! As a financial supplement, my father and uncle started a cognac home brewing business by distilling cheap Italian wine, mixing the alcohol obtained with water and cognac extract (burned sugar and extract), and refilling empty English clear glass beer bottles. These we affixed with fancy locally printed cognac labels and sold to the local bars. The British military loved our home brew and business was good for a short while.

Around this time my Grandfather and Uncle (who had married a great Italian lady) decided to go back to Yugoslavia, but my father's stipulations were not accepted by the new Yugoslav government. We opted not to return home and moved to Rome.

We remained in Rome for seven years. My Dad managed a light bulb and battery factory in Rome (Sole); my mother visited with her old friends from Zagreb who also had opted to remain in Italy, and my sister and I went to school. My sister went to the French School in Rome, while I was shipped to a school in Frascati, the Villa Collegio Mondragone, run by the Jesuits. I guess my parents thought I needed more discipline! Mondragone was an old palace of the popes, built in 1573, where Pope Gregory XIII signed the present Gregorian calendar in 1582. So much for history!

In 1951 we obtained permission to immigrate to the United States. We settled in Indianapolis where my father had obtained an engineering position with RCA. My sister and I completed high school in Nap Town (what we called Indianapolis), and both of us went to Purdue University and graduated in due time. My own time at Purdue was interrupted for two years "working" for Uncle Sam. I was fortunate to serve at Fort Ord in California and, later, in Puerto Rico.

When I returned to Purdue, I pursued a lovely co-ed, Jan, who happened to live in the sorority house across the street from my fraternity. As luck would have it, she decided to share my sentiments and, on her day of graduation, we tied our marital knots and moved to Schenectady, New York where I was completing the last two years of my three-year stint in the GE Management Training Program.

We moved around the country for the next two years, on various GE assignments, and eventually settled in Utica, New York, still with GE. During this period my wife worked as a Speech and Hearing Therapist in various schools and hospitals. After thirteen years, two children and two homes later, we left Utica and GE, and moved to Medford, New Jersey, where I had joined GTE Information Systems. Eventually, in about two years, GTE had an opening in Mountain View, California. We jumped at the opportunity and moved to Los Gatos where we built a house and settled down.

My tenure with GTE was short and I found myself working for Intel's Development Systems Division. That was an exciting period of time, given the dynamic nature of a growing and expanding Intel, their unique management style, and their high tech products. During this period we built a second home, this time on a hill in Monte Sereno, to gain access to the Los Gatos schools for our children and more privacy for us. (The first home, while in Los Gatos, had required that they attend the Campbell High School.)

When my Intel division relocated in Oregon and Arizona and our hearts were still attached to California, I joined Northern Telecom in Santa Clara, and eventually took a job with Metricom, a technology start -up, located in Los Gatos. My 40-minute traffic intensive commute became traffic-free with a duration of less than seven minutes! The products we made were very high tech, innovative, and challenging, in the new wireless communication and smart electricity metering field. Our management team was very cohesive, focused, and challenged. We were the first company that could, and did, provide wireless and Internet connections over large city areas, to mobile and stationary computers and devices.

During this period Jan obtained an advanced degree in Art History and started to teach at several local colleges. Her teaching demanded a vast supply of photo slides of art and antiquities from many civilizations over many centuries. To satisfy this need, we started to travel extensively to Europe for our vacations, visiting and photographing historical landmarks which included art works in most European museums and buildings. Over a 15-year period she accumulated over 22,000 slides, some purchased and some of objects photographed by us.

At the same time our two boys finished high school, graduated from colleges, and moved out of our home. One of them married and had two boys; both purchased their homes, settling down locally in Los Altos and San José.

Pretty soon I reached the magic age when I had planned on retiring and left the challenges of new products, intensive management, and long hours. I switched to washing dishes, vacuuming the house, fixing home problems, polishing my cars, and more extensive travel. My wife decided to stop her teaching career and we became pupils again, attending classes and seminars and expanding our travels.

Eventually owning and attending to a large home became less of a priority and we started to address the issues of post-retirement life. We soon selected the Saratoga Retirement Community as our next stop. After a three-year wait, we finally were called and given the opportunity to occupy a cottage in that community. In the meantime we had sold our home and somehow packed ourselves into a much smaller rental apartment, where we survived for five months.

It has now been two and one-half years since we moved into our cottage at SRC, but it seems to us as if we had just moved in one year ago. We enjoy the people, the facility, the services, and the location, as well as the various programs offered, the socializing, and the food. We are extremely comfortable with our choice and our situation.

Chanel No. 5

Judith Oppenheimer

My uncle Robert handed me a
small package wrapped in flowery paper.
I opened it to find a large bottle of Chanel No. 5.
I ran my fingers down the bottle's
Smooth graceful surface.
The transparent liquid caught
the light like an amber sunset.
What a strange gift for an eleven-year-old ranch girl!
Where would I use it?
I dabbed droplets on my cheeks, my neck,
walked to the barn where
Its sweet, fresh scent mingled with
the loamy aroma of
hay, cattle and
the manure carpet of the barn.
I kept the bottle of tawny liquid,
used it occasionally when I went
to a play, a concert.
At fortysomething
I threw away the almost full bottle.
I forgot its fragrance, its allure,
but the mystery still remained.

Was this a gift for an early Bat Mitzvah,
a celebration of my young womanhood?
Did this man who led the Manhattan Project,
who seemed so aloof,
who often could only touch his own children
while leaning over a couch or a chair as a barrier,
see what my parents couldn't see?

Tales from Oz

Horace Osgood Hayes

I am descended from two pioneer families—the Osgoods and the Hayes. The Osgood family on my mother's side came to the United States on the third ship after the *Mayflower.* They settled in Blue Hill, Maine. That ancestor, who was an undertaker during the Revolutionary War, makes me a member of the *Order of Revolutionary Descendants.* SRC's Independent Living Marketing Director, Susan Peterman, has a maiden name –Osgood—in the same family tree so we trace our ancestors together. Further down the tree, when George Washington founded his first Cabinet, Christopher Osgood was named the first Postmaster General. That puts me in the *Order of Founders and Patriots.* Both these Orders are among those listed in the Social Register.

The Hayes family came from County Ireland to Honesdale, Pennsylvania and from there by covered wagon to California in 1830. This was before California became a state in 1850 when, at the same time San Francisco became incorporated as a city, Hayes Street was named for my ancestor, Thomas, the first County Clerk in San Francisco. He had the great advantage of knowing who couldn't pay their tax bills. This gave him the opportunity to purchase all the land from Market to Golden Gate Park for seven cents an acre. At that time it was all sand dunes! Thomas' home was built at the corner of Hayes and Van Ness where the Davies Symphony Hall is today. His brother, Timothy Hayes, settled in Livermore and eventually formed the Wente Brothers Winery before we sold it to them. His son, also Timothy, and my grandfather moved to Visalia, California and eventually purchased seven ranches which amounted to about 10,000 acres. He raised beef and dairy cattle, wheat, corn, and, in recent times, cotton. We had several ranches in the San Joaquin Valley. The other ones were down in Visalia in southern California. They took a great deal of my time, not farming them, but managing them. So I didn't have the opportunity to devote myself to the piano that I would have liked.

I was born in San Francisco in 1933 and, in adolescence, went to Lowell High School. My mother was an opera singer and I inherited her musical ability. I wanted to be a concert pianist. My father, Horace, was a famous football player at Berkeley on what, in 1915, they called "The Wonder Team" under Andy Smith. He didn't want his son to be a concert pianist! (My sister became the family athlete—a basketball player.) So my grandmother paid for my piano lessons and, when I was 17 years old, I played in the Opera House in San Francisco in the Young People's Orchestra under Rudolph Ganz. I played the Schumann *Piano Concerto in A Minor.* I won a scholarship to U. C. Berkeley and would have stayed if that school hadn't been so big. I transferred to Duke University in Durham, North Carolina where I started as a pre-med student and then changed my major to European History and Musicology to get my Bachelor's Degree. From there I went to Graduate School at Yale, studying Musicology.

Joining the Army voluntarily in 1959, I got the chance to choose where I went. That was to Colorado Springs, Colorado, a two-year active commitment. After that, I joined the Wells Fargo Bank International Department and was appointed Banking Officer aboard the Matson ship *Mariposa* for two years, sailing from San Francisco to Tahiti, then to New Zealand and Australia, and back to San Francisco by way of the Hawaiian Islands.

After leaving the ship, I was put in charge of its future bankers. Then, unfortunately, my mother and father died within a month of each other. My aunt also died within another month and I became Trustee of eight family trusts. At this time I got seriously interested, on a volunteer basis, with the Merola Opera Program of the San Francisco Opera where I was on the Board for 30 years. I was also involved with the Metropolitan Opera Auditions and founded the Vocal Arts Foundation to finance those auditions in northern California. I did this for 30 years, too.

One of my more successful enterprises occurred when I had my home in Marin County. I held musicales there which were devoted to old operatic phonographic records. By that time I had a very famous collection. I had started collecting when I was about ten years old and, when I was older, what I would do to share that collection was to devote an evening to the singers of what was called the *Golden Age of Opera*, people like Nellie Melba, Enrico Caruso, and Luisa Tetrazzini. I would read a short biography of each singer and play recordings at the appropriate time during the reading. Then there would be a dinner based on the food pleasures of the particular singer I was featuring. I found the recipes in books about the singers. At these musicales I would sometimes play with a violinist or in a chamber music selection.

I also had, and still have, a collection of books and biographies to do with the famous singers of the Golden Age. There are also autographed photographs signed to me, and extremely valuable. (The one of Caruso has a price of over $10,000.) Most of these records and biographies I have donated to Stanford University and to the Archives of Recorded Sound. I worked as a volunteer at the Archives for seven years and, when their donations included artifacts that they already had, I was given them. These gifts often doubled in value after I owned them.

I was in touch with many famous collectors around the world, such as Francis Robinson who was the Vice-President of the Metropolitan Opera. We used to exchange records. Another one was Lord Harewood in England. We also discussed records and I visited several times at his home which is one of the treasure houses of England. I believe it is one owned by the National Trust and is what is referred to as a Stately Home.

At any rate, that was one of my many collections. They all had to do with music. A large collection of mine was the phonographs themselves. I had all of the early cylinder phonographs of Edison who invented the phonograph. Edison's daughter invited me to her home in Montclair, New Jersey to thank me for the collection. She also gave me a photograph of her father with his invention. I had the early models of the Victrola all the way up to the first electric version. They were shown at the Old Mint which is on Fifth and Mission in a whole room devoted to my collection. I had all the phonographs in there for people to view. Today the government, for economic reasons, has discontinued the museum.

These areas and enterprises took most of my time, collecting and going to see people's collections. I took some good items from their libraries. As far as the phonographs are concerned, since they are electrical and have much better sound now, people wanted to dispose of their Victrolas and so forth. I got some very good bargains of very rare machines. So that is pretty much the extent of my collecting.

But I do have a small collection of clocks—cuckoo clocks and ship clocks that I displayed in the cases in the Manor at the Saratoga Retirement Community. In fact, many examples of my collections have been displayed in the Manor showcases from time to time. I welcome comments or questions about what is there.

My Nursing Career

Sheila Gault

I was born in a small town in Manitoba, Canada and lived on a farm until I started my nursing training in Winnipeg, Manitoba in the same hospital from which my mother graduated from her nurse's training. (She endured the 1918 flu epidemic.) Our hospital was called Misericodia General and had been built in 1915. The three-year program ended with my graduating in a class of forty as a Registered Nurse (RN).

Training to become a medical professional was different in those days. (One thing may not have changed: fainting at the first sight of blood.) We were a very close group of students who had reunions about every five years until we arrived at our 50th anniversary in 1999 in Winnipeg. When we met to commemorate our earlier training, we put together an informative booklet about our shared experience.

The most important goal of the program was reached after three months when we were given our caps. These caps were used as a means of punishment and reward. If mistakes or any infraction of the rules took place, we had to remove our caps and felt real shame when we had to go on wards without them. Some of the girls quit after that, especially the ones who weren't used to hard farm work. The reward for doing well was that the caps were a clear indication of how far we had come in our studies. After the first year we received a light blue band; after the second, that was replaced by a dark blue one, and when we graduated we were given the coveted black band.

Some of the memories of that time at the Misericordia focused on our meals. Breakfast provided crusty rolls with figs or prunes. In our last year came jam and a scoop (one) of ice cream on Sundays. Everybody remembers our glasses of milk with an inch of salt peter around the rim. (I think that was intended to delay our libido.) The students and graduate nurses ate in separate dining rooms, lined up to get our meals, eat, clean our utensils in the sink, and put them away in our own cubicle. All that in half an hour! What I remember about dinner was meatballs, liver and onions, Shepard's pie, sauerkraut, jelly, and fish croquettes. We really appreciated working in the Diet Kitchen where the interns came to the door for their meals and we had the chance to stuff our mouths full when Sister wasn't looking. (We all wore bibs into which we stuffed bananas when she wasn't looking, too.)

The doctors we worked with in the Operation Room (OR) were both admired and feared. But one reason we liked being assigned to work there was the chance to take a real shower when we were on a call. First timers were sent for a circumcision mask. During one of Dr. Shepard's gastrostomies one of us kicked a sponge bucket by accident. But one of the most embarrassing times of all was when the doctor asked any newcomer to hand him "a monkey on a stick." Who knew what that was? (It turned out to be an instrument with a sponge at one end for dabbing on a wound.) When a certain doctor asked for a spoon, one of us handed him a sterile one. He exploded and she learned quickly that "spoon" was his word for a small curette.

We eight "cellar rats" lived in the basement of Cornish Court which was torn down in the 80s. After lights out we'd get together in one room, drink tea, and howl at our own jokes. We especially enjoyed our made-up definitions of essential medical terms like these:

Artery	Study of paintings
Bacteria	Back door to the cafeteria
Caesarean Section	A district in Rome
Enema	Not a friend
Labour Pain	Getting hurt at work
Outpatient	Patient who has fainted
Terminal Illness	Getting sick at the airport
Urine	Opposite of you're out!

(When I remember the use of words, here's another one. There was once a handsome young priest who was a patient in a private room on "Obstets" who said that he was the only father on the ward.)

The black iron bars on our basement windows came in handy when the police warned us about a "peeping Tom" who had been seen in the area exposing himself. Once a mean joke was played on Norma who everybody knew had a dreadful fear of cats. She climbed into bed and found the residence cat had been placed there before her.

King George and King Edward Hospitals were for communicable disease patients. We loved going there not just because we liked the wonderful matron, Ms. Shepherd, but because the grounds were beautiful and the food a treat. We contacted the Navy barracks to get men to come to a dance. It was a scary time, though, before the Salk vaccine. We treated two girls in iron lungs. What they got was hot foments every quarter of an hour or sooner. There was no known cure.

My training began in 1946 and ended in 1949 when we graduated and were prepared to become practicing nurses in the field. My first year was spent in Vancouver in the Operating Room at St Paul's Hospital. While I was there, I took a post-graduate study in Orthopedic Surgery in the Operating Room. Then I went to work for the Sisters in a small hospital on Vancouver Island. It was north of Victoria in an area called Campbell River. I spent one year there before moving to Providence Hospital in Seattle. There were two of us working there who already had jobs in Honolulu but, in order to receive our citizenship, it was easier not to wait to go there but to get it through jobs in Seattle.

One year later, since I desired to travel more, I took a position in Albuquerque, New Mexico where I spent five wonderful years in the Operating Room. I was married and my son, Robert, was born there. After my husband graduated from the University of New Mexico we traveled various places for Westinghouse, ending up In Houston, Texas where I worked in the Operating Room at M. D. Anderson Hospital for six months. Then came my husband's desire to move to Palo Alto, California with Lockheed.

My nursing career ended for seventeen years while raising my son and a daughter, Sheryl.

We bought our first home in San José and had a marvelous neighborhood to bring up our children in. My husband, by then with IBM, was transferred to New York for two years. We returned to San José in 1968 where I was still not doing any nursing until 1974 when West Valley College began a refresher course in Operating Room Nursing. After one semester on-the-job training, I took a post at Good Samaritan in the Operating Room where I worked until I retired until 1994.

I specialized in orthopedic nursing, assisting the doctors in two ways: scrubbing and circulating—that is, putting sterile gowns and gloves on them and making available the sterilized instruments and implants that were needed for each operation. After I retired, I helped my son select various surgical instruments for sale. He was the representative for various companies in the orthopedic business and I continued my interest in orthopedics, helping my son to supply a wide range of instruments for hips, knees, shoulders, and other body parts.

Some interests never disappear. I'm glad I chose nursing for my career. It gave me great satisfaction to help take care of patients and meet wonderful people doing the same thing.

As Time Goes By

Jerry Daniels

The nineteen thirties and forties were my years of growing up in the Bronx, New York. My two brothers were 14 and 11 years older than I was, so I really didn't know them well during my youth. My sister was five years older, too.

This age gap with my siblings meant that I felt like an only child. My Dad died when I was eleven, so from then on I was raised by my mother. I don't know if this youthful background was the reason for my memory vacuum about my life until I started college. All prior recollection seems like a complete blank to me. My mother came from the Sephardic tradition with beliefs that feelings should be kept private. My parents spoke mostly Ladino, their native tongue. That was until my older brother started elementary school speaking little English. Very embarrassed, he came home and cried to our parents, convincing them to speak mostly English to their children from then on.

I was a loner, even after starting my New York University engineering studies within walking distance from my home in a five-story apartment building. I didn't participate in campus social life since I went back home to be with my Mom and concentrate on my studies. I wanted to study electrical engineering, but I was amazed to discover that I saw numbers in a color test that the other students with normal color recognition didn't observe. My blindness was confirmed when I tried to read the color bands on electrical resistors and failed miserably. Oh well, mechanical engineering would be ok with me.

I graduated from high school in 1948, just as the war veterans were returning home and enrolling in college. I was an honors student in high school and I thought

I was "king of the hill." It would be a breeze to compete with the GIs who had not been in school but fighting in World War II. What a shock! Competing with these older mature students turned out to be extremely challenging. Many were married and had kids, so their motivation to study and get good grades was very high. Grading on tests was on a curve and I found myself on the curve's low end, an embarrassing state of affairs. It took my freshman year to recover from that "competition shock" and realize that I had to work and study harder against these older, and highly motivated, mature guys in my class.

ROTC (Reserve Officer Training Corps) at NYU was compulsory for the first two years, so there I was in my soldier suit marching across the parade grounds. One of the members of my platoon was a recent immigrant from Greece who didn't speak English well. He had trouble with the various commands. The rest of us would be in stitches as he shouted out, "RIGHT FLANK...GO!", or "TO THE REAR, HO!" He had a good sense of humor and laughed along with us. Our platoon leader wasn't too happy about these antics, but somehow we all survived the two years of soldier interaction.

ROTC was also offered as an optional course for the last two undergraduate years. It was made attractive by providing a stipend and other incentives. I was more eager to acquire technical courses in engineering, so I decided not to enroll in this advanced ROTC. This turned out to be a life-saving decision since a number of my friends continued on with the program and were sent to Korea with the rank of Second Lieutenant and a minimum of hard training. They led other poorly trained troops into battle and some of them were killed or wounded. That was a lucky decision on my part since I had no inkling that the Korean war was still raging with no end in sight.

In my senior year at NYU a number of companies sent recruiters to our campus. In 1951, the year I graduated, there were jobs available and the competition between companies to hire students was keen. I thought I would go directly into an engineering job, but I really had no idea what to look for. I was surprised and pleased when Westinghouse offered me a job with the opportunity to enter their Graduate Student Training Program headquartered in Pittsburgh, Pennsylvania. I may not have had any idea about what I was getting into, but it turned out to be one of the most important life-changing moments in my working career.

I had lived alone with my mother and was reluctant to leave her, but she encouraged me to take the offer even though it meant being away from home for at least a year. Mom was from the "old school: and her only words of advice as I departed to Pittsburgh were to be careful. (Whatever did that mean? I knew the answer: no contact with girls, no sex education.)

There I was, 21 years old and for the first time out of New York and living at a boarding house, ready to take on an adventure into the corporate world. It began with a few weeks of orientation at the Graduate Student Training Center, then a year's worth of assignments in different manufacturing plants where I was exposed to a variety of disciplines. This was a fascinating and exciting time, delving into quality control, design engineering material testing, welding, and even marketing. What a great way to help me to decide the direction I would like to take for my life-long career in manufacturing! I felt as if I had a bright future and the whole world was my oyster.

I accepted a position at the Meter Division in Newark, New Jersey. In that way I could live in New York with my mother and commute to work. I became an Assistant Foreman in the Punch Press Department where we made parts for watt-hour meters and other electrical instruments. That the plant was the oldest in the company was obvious when I saw the overhead belt-driven machines and ancient equipment turning out parts for modern electrical instruments. I felt as if I were in a time machine going back at least a hundred years.

Because we were making some instruments used by the Defense Department, I was able to get a deferment from my Draft Board. But they finally caught up to me two years later and, in 1954, I was drafted. After a grueling few months in Basic Training at Fort Dix, I was assigned to Camp Detrick in Frederick, Maryland. That was a secret facility involved with biological weapons research. I discovered when I came to the Saratoga Retirement Community that my mentor and neighbor, Lee Wilson, was at this same research facility at exactly the same two-year period. Both of us were drafted GIs.

Initially I was assigned to the Safety Engineering Group. But before entering any of these "hot" buildings where experiments were conducted to find antidotes for a variety of diseases, I was required to take inoculations to protect myself from these unfriendly germs. These included anthrax, tularemia, and eastern equine encephalitis. All very scary indeed! Fortunately, an offer came just in time for me to work in the Procurement Department where my job was to assist in negotiating contracts with outside companies. I was greatly relieved not to have to work with "hot" stuff.

Only a few months after we married, my wife, Esther, was able to join me in Maryland. Being married gave me the opportunity to live off-campus. I felt as if I really weren't in the Army, but in a civilian job environment. I even played on the camp's tennis team and travelled to many different military installations in Maryland, Washington, D.C., and Virginia. I thought I was very lucky to be able to spend my Army days in that way.

After my two-year stint in the Army I had another life-changing experience. That was driving across the country as part of my terminal leave. My first view of the Pacific Ocean, visiting family in Portland, Oregon and seeing San Francisco, aroused the desire to live in this enchanted part of the country.

However, I returned to my job at the Westinghouse Meter Division. The plant was on its last legs, the building showing the wear and tear of almost a hundred years' existence. In 1959 Management finally made the decision to close the facility and move to Raleigh, North Carolina. Recalling my west coast trip, I elected to request a transfer to the Steam Turbine division in Sunnyvale, California. Luck was with me and my little family, which included our one-year-old daughter, Audrey, made the most important move of my lifetime.

For me, for the next 32 years, excluding a few minor excursions, Westinghouse was the source of exciting and innovating experiences. The 1960s stand out as a time when I was Project Manager for the design and construction of a 130-foot diameter radio telescope, the largest moving instrument in the world. It was exciting to be associated with astronomers and research people from the California Institute of Technology, our customer for this program. The dish was too big to be made and shipped from our plant, so it was built in sections and welded together at the final site, the Owens Valley Observatory on the other side of the High Sierras. Many design and manufacturing challenges needed to be met, but we achieved our goal.

I became involved with the Sunnyvale Junior Chamber of Commerce during the early 1960s and spent a year as President of our local branch. We worked on a variety of city planning activities and made many new friends. I was reluctantly forced into retirement from the club when I turned 35 and became what was known in the organization as an "exhausted rooster."

My daughter, Audrey, was almost old enough to attend Hebrew school, but there were no conservative Jewish congregations in the Sunnyvale/Saratoga area. I got together with a few of my new friends and discussed possible alternatives. With a nucleus of four families willing to start a new synagogue, we jumped into the unknown territory of a religious "start-up congregation." With no start-up money, just a lot of enthusiasm, we incorporated and founded Congregation Beth David in 1963. We weren't sure what to do first, but we knew we needed to elect officers and start having services. At a late night meeting we went around the room trying to decide who would do what job. Nobody wanted the one of President and the group became quiet and contemplative. Then they all looked at me and by acclamation (and under mild protest), I became the founding President of our fledgling congregation. With very little money we hired a part-time rabbi and started conducting services in churches or halls that we could rent for the few dollars we had collected. I recall vividly one special service, the evening after President Kennedy was killed. The building we were renting was very small, but we amassed an overflow crowd to pray on a rainy and dismal night. We were able to secure the services of the rabbi from San Quentin jail to conduct this somber and moving prayer session.

Congregation Beth David has been an important part of our family life. In 1973 we acquired land next to the Church of Ascension and built our first real permanent home. We celebrated our fifty year anniversary in 2013 with a series of special events.

My little family moved from Sunnyvale to Saratoga in 1966. After a brief period of time exploring other business opportunities, I decided to return to Westinghouse, spending my last ten years as Program Manager of a high-power laser facility. The corporation funded us to develop manufacturing applications for all divisions across the country. To be involved with a new and important technology was a dream come true. I felt like a kid with a new toy, anxious to go to work every day to explore the incredible possibilities for advanced manufacturing processes. This dream job lasted until I reluctantly retired in 1993.

My wife and I started to explore ways to expand our horizons. We found an organization called Jewish Marriage Encounter (JME), introduced to us by a member of our Congregation. The purpose was to find ways to enhance our relationship, even though we were wary of the use of the name "Encounter." The concepts and the new friendships we made enriched our lives. Meeting monthly with this new group of friends in a secure and warm environment was a revelation. It became an important part of our lives.

When Esther died five years ago, I was devastated and lonely. But it was my very good fortune that same year to find a woman who was a member of Congregation Beth David when we were both mourning the loss of our spouses. We have since become "forever fiancés" and continue to treasure our lives together.

The Dream

Betty Bocks

Both of these memories began with a vivid dream in my 80s, a dream that brought back a loving relationship long locked away when it was permanently lost. From there the memories went on quite on their own into more of the past still with me today.

The first was a dream that awoke me, amazed and weeping. My stomach was in a turmoil. In that dream, I was six years old, in the first grade at Hester School when the recess bell rang. I was always the first out the door, running madly ahead to claim one of the three swings in the playground. When I hopped off to give someone else a turn, a little girl in my class came up to me and said, "Did you know your sister is killed?" The speaker's name was Jane and she was a tattletale kind of child, so I said," No, she isn't!" and walked away.

But Jane was right. She knew what she was saying. My beautiful sister, my hero, my Ginny, was dead. She was nine years old and in the fourth grade and we had walked to school on that October morning kicking leaves the way we always did. She would run ahead of me, teasing, then slowing while my shorter legs caught up. I loved her. We slept together and traded secrets and she was my whole world.

Soon after my father came to school and took me home where my mother was lying on her bed. Her face was all red, as much as I could see. My little brother, four-year-old Raymond, was sobbing beside her and his face was all red, too. My father went outside, sat down on the porch steps, and lit his pipe. I went out there, too, and sat down with him. He didn't say anything and I didn't, either. I don't know how long we sat there, but the word had spread without our doing anything about it. People started coming to see us. My mother had taught me how to greet guests and I went to the door to meet them. I invited them in and tried to find the hostess words that my mother used, but soon, except for my grandparents, everyone was gone, anyway. My grandmother gathered me into her arms, but I wiggled so much that she let me go. So I sat on the floor in the corner of the living room and she went to see if she could help my mother. My brother who was only four lay on his stomach on the floor and tried to read a comic book. My grandfather tried to begin making conversation, but he soon stopped. No one spoke.

Two days later an older girl, a neighbor, came and took me to her house and we played some games for a while. Then we went out to sit on the front porch. While we were there, we saw an ambulance stopping In front of our house. The new arrivals pulled out a stretcher and went into the building. When they came out, I saw my sister lying on it. I could see her legs; they were all bandaged. I started to run down there to see her more closely, but my friend held me back. She said, "Your mother is going to dress Ginny for the funeral tomorrow and you will see her then." I sat down again and tried not to cry. The next day my grandmother dressed me in the twin dress that matched the one that Ginny was wearing that day. She was lying in the casket in front of the fireplace in the living room, looking beautiful and asleep. Her long curly hair was brushed and her bangs, neat. She had always been such a bundle of activity that I couldn't believe how still she was.

I went out to the garden and picked a flower and my grandmother told me to put it next to Ginny. Then she held me up and told me to kiss my sister "Goodbye!" I did that and then went out and sat on the back steps, numb and silent.

That night, when I was lying in bed, I heard the backdoor open and swing shut. Then I heard my mother crying in the dark garden. I thought of Ginny. I was so lonely without her beside me, that I spread my fingers and ran my hand over the sheet next to me. A warm, soft, little hand reached out and clasped mine.

Even by three years later, when I was nine years old, I had never talked about my sister or when she left us. She was nine when she had been killed by that truck on the Alameda in San José right in front of the Hester School where she was in the fourth grade. Afterwards nobody in the family ever talked about her, so I decided I wouldn't, either. So I didn't.

I played with my friends and the years went by. When I was nine, the neighbor girls and I decided we would have a spring entertainment for our parents and planned to have it at the neighbors. They had a sloping lawn in their back garden which would be a natural stage. I thought I would do a dance in the performance and wear a dress that I had worn before at a recital. It was a pale green Tarleton net with layers on the bouffant skirt and pink roses strewn all over. A neighbor boy took back the flashlight he had loaned us to light our surroundings and someone brought us a lighted candle and placed it on the rung of the fence to replace the flashlight. When I moved closely by it, my full dress spread like leaves over it and burst into flames! I took off as fast as I could into the street, hoping to get away from the fire. A man driving a cleaner's truck saw me running covered with flames and stopped his truck to get out a blanket. He rolled me up in it and put out the smothered fire.

By this time I was unconscious. I stayed that way until I was deposited in a neighbor's house. The woman there was a registered nurse who smeared butter all over my body. It felt to me as if I were going to be barbecued! I don't think I cried because I was so numb I couldn't even do that. But that was only the beginning. The healing that began then took a long time. I laid on my stomach in a little round tent with a light hanging inside. I couldn't turn over. My back and my under arms were huge puddles of pain; my legs were in the same shape. The doctor and the nurse came every day bringing me codeine. Perhaps it helped me sleep, but it didn't stop the hurting. Most days my mother changed my dressings herself. My friends didn't come to visit me but their mothers did and brought flowers. We had flowers all over my room! They smelled lovely even if I smelled terrible.

It was a painful recovery for me, one that took a long time—six months for the first- and second-degree burns to heal and almost a year for the third degree ones. They were the ones on my arms and my back which my father and mother rubbed with cocoa butter every night until I was a teenager. That was when I wouldn't let them do it anymore. I was very sensitive about my scars, even covering my body when I went swimming or began dancing again. It took many years before I stopped being aware of them and trying to hide them. I assumed I would never have a boyfriend because I was so badly scarred. That was a real blow.

All through the years since her death I had deliberately kept my beloved sister out of my thoughts, but when I was lying there in my tent, unable to stop hurting or even to turn over, Ginny would creep in and join me. Her presence was comforting, but I hurt so much that I wondered if she would stop coming—if I would die and join her in Heaven.

Today I am 92, healthy and active. The rest of my life is yet to be told.

A Dam Story

Kutlu Enver Doluca

Walking in galleries of Grand Coulee Dam, a massive large concrete gravity structure on Columbia River in Washington State, in 1952, I touched a water level checking sensor. That triggered water level control pumps in the galleries. They operated for one minute. The noise in the galleries was so high that I had to grab my guide's arm. He was an engineer of the Bureau of Reclamation (USBR), a Federal Government Agency responsible for the majority of Dam and Hydroelectric Projects in U.S. Western States. It was one of the happiest times of my life when I was assigned to take training in-service with USBR for one year.

My passion for dams started when I was sent to the orchard of my Granddad and Grandma at the age of 14 in a small town 80 miles north of Ankara, the capital of Turkey. The gardens were on sloped land. There were two main irrigation ditches crossing the gardens. Elevation of one ditch was about 30 feet higher than the other one. During the three months I stayed at the orchard, I built a side connection from the upper ditch to the lower one. On this connection I built a small wooden dam, creating a small pond. I made a small wooden waterwheel and placed the wheel under a waterfall from the pond. This waterwheel operated during my stay. Because I enjoyed this experience very much, 1 decided to become a civil engineer and deal with dams and hydroelectric projects. After graduation from the Technical University of Istanbul, I applied to the Turkish Government Agency responsible for research and development of hydroelectric power projects (EIE Administration) in 1949. For EIE, I surveyed sites for hydroelectric power projects in Turkey.

The EIE Administration included me in a group of five engineers to participate in a training program of ECA (Economic Cooperation Agency) of the State Department in 1952. ECA was one of the departments established under the Marshall Plan to help underdeveloped countries after the Second World War.

After arriving in Denver in May 1953, I was sent to Hungry Horse Dam which was under construction near Glacier National Park in Montana. On the way there I was given an extensive tour of Grand Coulee Dam.

I stayed three months at the Hungry Horse Dam construction, one that is a 564-feet high concrete arch dam on Flat Head River. (This dam and the hydroelectric power plant were completed in 1953.) I was assigned to aggregate inspection in the first month. Gradation of aggregate is very important in concrete dams to improve their strength. I checked the gradation before it was sent to batch plant. The second month I was an inspector there at batch plant. There were five mixers. Aggregate, cement, and water came there by belt conveyors and were put in mixers. The amounts of each ingredient were checked by automatic weight control devices. Strength of concrete may change considerably on the basis of the amount of each ingredient used. Several concrete mixes are designed for different purposes depending on where the finished product will go. The design is made by extensive laboratory tests beforehand. At the batch plant my duty was to take samples from mixers and send them to our laboratory for checking.

During my last month there my assignment was on the dam itself. I was an inspector who ordered concrete to be placed in blocks from the batch plant and watched the pouring of concrete in blocks of the dam. A concrete arch dam is built block by block with five-foot height. Before placing each additional block, it is necessary to sandblast the surface of the previous block to secure water tightness. Kalispell, Montana was the closest city to the dam site where I was working. Its population was around 20,000 in 1952. I used to go there during weekends. White Fish, Montana was nearby, an even smaller town with recreational facilities. A ski resort was built there on Big Mountain. It was possible to see beautiful Flathead Valley from the top of that mountain. I went to Big Mountain twice when there was no snow. It was very pleasant to look at Flathead Valley and all the greenery around. Beautiful Glacier National Park is four miles from Hungry Horse Dam. I visited this park twice, too. Half of this park is in the United States and other half is in Canada. I went to the part in Montana three times and enjoyed the scenery and facilities very much. I returned to Denver, Colorado in September of 1952 and stayed in USBR offices there for four months. During this period my assignment was designing a concrete cooling system for a gravity dam. After placing, concrete generates heat for an extended time. If not cooled, this heat can cause cracks in the concrete. Cooling is achieved by placing pipes and circulating water in concrete blocks. Another method is to make concrete very cool by adding ice to it at the time of placing.

During my stay in Denver, I visited a number of interesting places around the city. Estes Park and Rocky Mountain National Park and the old city of Golden were among them. One of the trips I enjoyed was to Wray, a city in eastern Colorado almost at the border of Kansas. The reason for my visit was the opening ceremony of one of the irrigation projects of USBR. An USBR official guided me to this event. Then my host took me to a baseball game. That was the first time I watched the game. I also posed with beautiful beauty pageant ladies at the baseball field.

One time I was interviewed by a WOR radio hostess broadcasting in their studio in Denver. This was an exciting happening for me. Along with the interview, there was a coffee advertisement. I had never seen anything like that before. While I was in the city I bought the *Rocky Mountain News* daily. In that newspaper for the first time I saw stock price lists page after page. I was interested in the price of IBM stock. I saw a large IBM computer in a window when I was walking on Colfax Avenue. I was attracted to the idea of buying IBM shares but my income was not enough. My daily allowance was $8! This was enough for a five-cent Coca Cola or a 25-cent hamburger, but not for buying expensive IBM shares! However, I did not forget this inclination. Years later when we moved to Seattle in 1982, I bought those shares along with others.

In January of 1953 USBR assigned me to Folsom and Nimbus dams near Sacramento, California and I had a chance to go to San Francisco during weekends where I spent most of my time in Golden Gate Park visiting museums. Then I was assigned to the Tecolote Tunnel construction of Cachuma Project at Santa Barbara, California. This was my third and last field assignment for USBR. I enjoyed living there in the beautiful month of April and took many slide pictures.

That stay played a big role in my final destination and my life. I was single when I was in service training in USBR in 1952. After I married in Turkey in 1956, we had two sons. I used to project the slides of my trip to the USA to my family from time to time. The ones of Santa Barbara had an impact on our sons. When they came to the USA for university education, both of them selected the University of

California at Santa Barbara and got their Masters degrees in Electrical Engineering there. When they were about to complete their studies, I advised them to get jobs in Silicon Valley which, in 1981, was in a hot developmental stage. Both of them were able to get jobs in electronic and technology companies and settled in Saratoga. Because they were there, I and my wife decided to move to the United States in 1982.

I accepted an offer from an engineering company having a branch office in Seattle, Washington. As our sons continued living in Saratoga, we moved into the Saratoga Retirement Community in 2011. I strongly believe that my staying in Santa Barbara and taking a lot of pictures there in 1953 had a definite impact on decisions made by members of our family. I spent my last month of ECA training period at the Detroit Edison Company in Detroit, Michigan. This time my object was to gather information on thermal power plants.

After returning to Turkey in May of 1953, I had a great chance to benefit from my experience with USBR: I was appointed as Head of Dams and Hydroelectric Power Plants at the Ministry of Public Works. The government was very eager to build dams to harness waterpower which was practically underdeveloped then. During my 32 years of professional work in Turkey I was involved with design and construction of 23 dams, two of which are as large as Hoover Dam.

On Becoming a Mother

Judith Oppenheimer

I was already in my 40s and we were discussing adoption one day when I drove home with a friend. She was playing the Devil's advocate for me: "Why not?" By the time I arrived I must have looked like a madwoman, simultaneously smiling and weeping.

I smiled because, for the first time in my life, I realized I did have something to give—my values, my warmth, my humanity.

I wept because I no longer felt that being a mother would be a selfish act, an act designed merely to ensure that someone would love me unconditionally. For the first time my dream of adopting a child seemed real and within my grasp.

I had always known that the only way I could become a mother was through adoption. I had flirted with the possibility several times before, but had never followed through. This time I was overcome with joy and certitude. How long it had been since I'd felt such a terrific sense of mission and passion!

I sank my bulldog perseverance into making my dream into reality. The next few weeks I flung myself at necessary action, whirling around my home and city with nonstop phone calls and visits. I called adoption agencies; I attended their orientations. I talked to my friends. All the women rejoiced with me. The only person I couldn't bring myself to tell was my father. Because I was to be a single parent the standard adoption agencies wouldn't even consider me for the adoption of an infant. I could have adopted an older child, a hard-to-place child, or a foreign one, but my heart was on a newborn. As a pediatrician, I had seen so many foster kids who had been moved from place to place and been abused. Even if they had warm, caring foster parents, by six months of age they often had been in two or more homes. I couldn't face having to undo harm that was already done.

I talked to my colleagues who were obstetricians and Emergency Room doctors. The mother of one of my patients, who had already adopted one child and was in the process of adopting another, gave me the name of her attorney, Mark Gradstein. He and his wife were well versed in the ins and outs of independent adoption which was not common then.

Early on the morning of December 17, 1982 an obstetrician called me at home. "I have a lady who just delivered a baby girl. I'm assigning the baby to you."

"Frazier, you didn't have to call me at home. I'm not on call. I'll see her in the morning."

"Judy, you misunderstood me. She's the lady I told you about some time ago. She still plans to place her baby up for adoption."

After he hung up, I did a little dance and shouted to the empty house. "Oh my God, I'm really going to be a mother!" I called Mark and rushed off to be with my petite, red-haired, blue-eyed daughter, Gabriele Jacquenette Oppenheimer.

My friend, Barbara Floyd, raced to the nursery to be with me. We headed out for a celebratory lunch and then spent the rest of the afternoon on a shopping spree buying diapers, bottles, formula, and a myriad of other necessities for caring for a new baby. I rushed around in a kind of delirium so much that, during our spree, I left several bags full of new merchandise on the checkout counter. Barbara had to retrieve them. In fact, when I returned to the car after lunch, I realized I had left my purse behind. Barbara looked at me with one brow raised. She was worried about the way I had forgotten my purse and packages.

When I returned from shopping, I called my father, "Hi, Pa! You're a grandfather!" I heard him gasp, "What?"

"I have a little girl I'm going to adopt. Her name is Gabriele Jacquenette." To my amazement, he didn't miss a beat, never questioned my decision, or asked why I hadn't told him of my plans before. Instead his voice flowed, warm and animated, through the phone. "What a wonderful Christmas gift! I love her name. When will she be home?"

"Probably tomorrow."

"Milly and I will be right down. See you tomorrow!"

Gabriele came home when she was two days old. My father held her and played with her. He told me that, when I held the baby, he loved watching me, I looked so happy, so relaxed! I was relieved, in fact thrilled, that my father was looking at me with different eyes. He was accepting me in my new role.

Gabriele was a cuddly baby, easy to quiet by letting her sleep on my breast. I spent many hours just holding or watching her. I resented being on call or having to go to meetings. I wanted to spend every minute I could with my newborn daughter. Sitting with other mothers in my office, I was able, for the first time in my life, to enter a world I had thought I would never experience: a feminine, maternal world. Friends and patients' parents would ask, "Does being a pediatrician make you a better parent?"

"No," I would answer. "Being a parent makes me a better pediatrician."

Like any other new parent, I worried that Gabriele was not gaining enough weight, that she spit up too much. I wondered about her development. I adapted to these sleepless nights, the rite of passage thrust upon all parents of a newborn. Yet, for me, it felt like a gift. I found a kind of magical quality about quiet hours spent in the middle of the night with Gabriele. I loved the way her hands searched my face and massaged my breast.

These were feelings I often recounted to the harried mothers who came into my office with their newborns. It felt wonderful to be able to counsel them from immediate, powerful experience. "Enjoy the quiet of the early morning times with your baby. Nap during the day whenever your baby is sleeping. Housecleaning and other chores can wait."

I should have had some inkling that this euphoria was far too good to last. The birth parents, it turned out, were young and Mormon. Although I knew how strange it was for a Mormon couple to be giving their baby up for adoption, I'd assumed they had dealt with the grandparents and the church.

But they had not. When Gabriele was six weeks old, I was playing the piano while she slept in her bassinet by the fireplace. The phone rang.

"Judy, this is Mark. I am making the kind of phone call I hate most." He paused and I could hear something fatal in his silence. Not really wanting to know, I nonetheless had to ask.

"Mark, what is it?" There was another pause.

"Gabriele's parents want her back."

"Oh my God! Why?"

Mark told me that the couple had told their parents that the baby had died. But the grandfather had become suspicious and, when the social worker who was involved in Gabriele's adoption called, asking to speak to her father, the grandfather pretended to be his son. The social worker told him that they needed to find a time to get together and talk. Once the grandparents knew the baby had been placed for adoption they demanded that their son and daughter-in-law get her back.

Stunned and shaking, I murmured, "Isn't there anything we can do?"

"Not really. Until the papers are signed you have no legal rights."

The rest of the evening was a blur. I called friends who rushed to the house. My father talked to Mark and me. Mark and I talked to the birth mother. I poured out my heart as I told her how much I loved Gabriele, how much it hurt to lose her. I had hoped that by hearing my voice, my passion for the baby both she and the grandparents would relent, that a miracle would happen. I spent the last portion of the evening alternating being on the phone and holding Gabriele. I was crying and crying, wanting to bang my head to make this nightmare disappear. I whimpered about how unfair life was.

Gabriele and I spent much of the night on the living room couch basking in the warmth of a blazing fire. As she slept against my breast, I tried desperately to cope. All I could do was try to memorize her. For one last time, I reveled in her warmth, her baby smell, and her cuddliness. I fervently hoped the birth parents and the grandparents would think once more about their decision, that in the morning I would get a call from Mark saying they had decided it would be best for Gabriele if she stayed with me. Around two in the morning she and I moved into my bed where she continued to rest warmly and quietly against me. My mind stormed and lulled, stormed and lulled. After sobbing, the circular thinking again started. I would cry and then drift off into a restless sleep. I wondered how I was going to survive without Gabriele. I felt at that point that my entire life had consisted of broken promises. I longed to fight for her, but Mark had already told me I had no legal recourse. All hope disappeared.

The next morning I actually dragged my exhausted body to the nursery to examine the newborns. I looked at each of them, stupefied. How could it be fair that so many new Moms would experience wonders and difficulties in raising a child and I wouldn't? I had an almost uncontrollable impulse to shoot—one that would reverberate from the walls like the explosion of the first atomic bomb. I went home to spend my last afternoon with Gabriele and that night she went back to Bob and Barbara's office and back to her birth parents.

From time to time over the years I have thought about the different life Gabriele would have had if she had been my daughter. I only hope that the love she received during the first six weeks made a positive difference to her. In the aftermath the house was my tomb. There was no point in spending the night in the huge dark place that had been a sanctuary of joy and hope. I spent that night with friends, getting their emotional support and a little rest. The next morning everyone was telling me to go to the beach, to Hawaii. But I needed to go somewhere where there was a lot of noise and life and motion, somewhere like New York.

Three of us—my office staff, my nurse, and I—boarded the red-eye to New York City and I spent three packed, recuperative, days there. We stayed in a hotel on 56th Street right in the middle of downtown Manhattan. When we arrived early in the morning, the other two left me to go exploring the surroundings. I was exhausted and slept hard in spite of the thunderous wrecking ball demolishing the building next door. Periodically I would wake up, realize where I was, and pound the pillow as I drifted in and out of remembrances of Gabriele. Eventually I slept.

While we were there, we went to museums, saw *The Fantastics*, talked, and shopped. In the midst of the urban hubbub, tears kept reappearing. At some point I was able to tell myself, *Thank God it was only six weeks and not six months!*

When I returned, facing the newborn nursery still closed my throat; any baby in my office between newborn and four months old caused me to fight back the tears. The pain was still too great to allow me to talk about my deepest feelings to anyone, even my best friends. Gradually the searing, branding iron of pain lifted so that I could again allow myself to take the risk and go through a process that had the potential of being so emotionally suicidal. I was able to revise my letter to potential birth parents. I told everyone I was going to try to adopt one more time. This time I managed my expectations with strict control, deliberately keeping them much smaller. Feelings were relegated to the backburner. Having to minimize the emotional perils, I vowed to be more straightforward in trying to find out how serious the mother was. I was determined to minimize the risk of adopting.

Mark gave me the name of a teenager who was due to deliver the end of April or beginning of May. After talking both to Mark and the mother of the pregnant teenager, we all agreed I would become the adoptive mother. I was scheduled to meet this young woman when, suddenly and rapidly, things changed. On the morning of February 16, 1983, I was in an exam room with a patient when my nurse knocked on the door, telling me that the ER doctor was on the phone. I went into my consulting room assuming that he had a sick patient who needed to be admitted or whom he wanted a consult on. I lifted the phone.

"Yes, Larry, what do you have for me?"

"I have a lady who just walked into the ER in labor. She wants to give the baby up for adoption. Do you want to come to see her?"

In spite of my resolve not to become too excited, my heart was pounding as I replied, "Let me finish with this one patient and I'll be right over."

I went on automatic pilot as I examined my patient and, after what felt like an infinity, I rushed to the ER. Once there, I walked into the ER cubicle to see a scared young woman in labor. I felt like a ghoul or vulture as I told her, gently and soothingly, that I wanted to adopt her baby. Briefly, I outlined the story about Gabriele and explained that I could not go through such an experience again. She reassured me that she had no thoughts about changing her mind. I asked her some questions about prenatal care (she had had none), about drugs and alcohol use (she denied both.) My intuition told me this twenty-year-old woman was trustworthy and that her baby would be okay.

I was in the ER doctor's office when, at 8:03 p.m. he phoned me to say he had just delivered a baby boy. Even though I had chosen a name for a boy—Neal Andrew—I was somewhat subdued. I had envisioned a daughter, but after seeing this lanky, blond baby boy, I felt ecstatic. He was alive! He sucked in his lower chin as he looked all around, seeming to take everything in. In spite of my excitement I had to spend the night soul-searching to get used to the fact that I was going to be the mother of a son and not a daughter. Maybe a son would be better than a daughter. I wouldn't have any expectations about how our relationship should be. With a daughter, there would always be my relationship with my mother to deal with.

Neal came home with me when he was two days old. His mother drove away in the same dusty pickup she used to drive herself to the hospital. For the first two weeks, I took Neal with me to my office where he held court in my consultation room for a series of adoring fans. Neal's birth mother signed the adoption papers within ten days. Within six months of age, Neal legally became my son.

I was a mother again. This time the experience was calm, real, and grounded. This time it was for keeps.

For me, being Neal's Mom filled a huge void. From the time he was an infant every free moment I had was spent with him. Suddenly I had someone to care for, someone who depended on me. I continued to be thrilled to be able to talk with other mothers at the pediatrician's office. People often approached and started talking to me simply because I had a child with me. Just being able to nurture erased many of my self-perceptions of inadequacy. I was a woman and a mother. No longer was I as isolated as I had been.

Neal's first nanny was a young woman from Mexico. She talked to him freely in Spanish which, in a way, became his first language. He also took Spanish in school and, as a consequence, he is now quite fluent in the language. I remember I felt somewhat concerned when he still wasn't talking a lot at 18 months but, once he started, he never was silent again. It was hard leaving Neal with his nanny during the day, but evenings and weekends were ours. Watching him develop his own personality forced me to learn interpersonal skills I had never actively had to summon before. I had to learn to listen to him, accept him, and accommodate him. I found that I was able to do this intuitively.

From birth, Neal has been a strong "I can do it myself" child. As an infant, whenever he cried or was fussy, I tried to comfort him by picking him up and holding him close to my breast. I soon learned that this usually didn't work. Instead, I had to lay him down. Then he would slowly calm himself. This need to be by himself became even more apparent when he was two. We had just returned from Sausalito after my father's death. Neal was having a terrible afternoon with one temper tantrum after another. Finally I simply had him go into his room, telling him he couldn't come out until he calmed down. It took two or three trips back to his room before he was able to face the day again.

Three weeks later I was trying to change his diaper and he was hysterical. At last he looked up at me and, on his own, said, "Neal calm down. Go to room." We went into his room together and he immediately was peaceful again. His diaper was easily changed.

Slowly I began to accept that I was able to communicate with another human being in an intimate, caring, manner. I could be the adult in the situation. My confidence in being a mother soared. I enjoyed letting my maternal feelings rush to the surface. Neal was a blond-haired, charismatic, kid. His ability to connect with others began slowly to rub off on me. I enjoyed talking to the strangers who were captivated by him. I became less shy when opportunities arose for initiating conversations.

As he grew older, almost every weekend when I wasn't on call, Neal and I took off. We went to Monterey where we rode our bicycles, went to the Monterey Bay

Aquarium, or just walked around sightseeing. At other times we drove to San Francisco where we stayed in a hotel close to Union Square. We spent our time joyfully sampling from the smorgasbord of activities near us there: visiting FAO Schwarz, the Academy of Sciences, the zoo, or the Exploratorium. We also spent hours in our pool at home, paddling, floating, racing, or inventing new water games. He was a true water baby. By the time he was eight months old, he was swimming the width of the pool underwater. I remember feeling awe as I watched him bob up and down as he kicked his way across.

Plenty of deep conversation happened between us. In fact, I wasn't quite prepared for how early they'd begin. When he was about two and one-half years old, he had gone to visit friends while I attended a staff meeting. The family was composed of a mother and father and three children. That night when he came home, he announced with ringing determination, "When I meet my father, I'm going to kill him!"

I was stunned. I had expected this anger when he was a teenager but not at two years old. I asked him, "Why?" Of course I couldn't articulate it, but I could deduce the answer. He had witnessed the conventional nuclear family structure. Over the next week or so I noticed his play included a father figure whose voice (provided by Neal) sounded authoritative. One night, shortly after that pronouncement about killing his father, he came to my bed at three in the morning.

"Mom, some kids have Dads. I don't."

Quietly I agreed. Then I asked him how he felt about it.

"Happy!"

He explained that he thought a father would be mean. At last I said, "I'd like to have a partner and for you to have a Dad, but, honey, we just don't." He smiled as he looked at me and said, "Don't worry, Mom. That's how the cookie crumbles!"

We never lacked for exciting adventures together vacationing in the Bahamas, St. John, and the American Virgin Islands where we both learned to snorkel. We spent time in England and on the ranch in Colorado. From kindergarten through sixth grade, Neal participated in his school's performances, first as Peter Pan in his kindergarten play and then in the dance programs. At ten he studied ballet at the San José Dance Theater. I marveled at his physical grace and stage presence when he danced the kopek in *The Nutcracker*.

Naturally, we also never lacked for challenges, difficulties, and crossroads forcing us to grow and adjust. At five he entered kindergarten at Harker, a private school in San José. The first year he had a wonderful teacher, Jeanne Davey. Although I had read to him many nights, it never became a bedtime routine. Therefore, I was totally amazed when after eight days in kindergarten, he sat down to read me one of his books. He was well on the way to decoding our written language.

I came home one evening to find Neal on the couch in my bedroom, reading. He showed me what it was—a script for a play.

"Mom, guess what! Mrs. Davey is going to do *Peter Pan* with all the kindergarten kids!"

I hugged him. "Wow! That sounds neat!"

He smiled slyly as he looked at me. "Guess who's going to be Peter!" I made my face a portrait of puzzlement and curiosity and opened my mouth to begin guessing any number of wildly inappropriate names. Within seconds he could contain himself no longer.

"Me!"

In spite of his love of kindergarten and that special teacher, by third grade he told me that he hated school. Thinking it was a phase, I didn't take him too seriously. But by sixth grade. Neal had developed a serious school phobia. Regularly he would wake up Monday morning announcing he felt "Yucky."

On occasion he would throw up. Once he actually passed out. He developed a pattern in which he would hibernate under his blanket all day long. I began to realize that, if he announced that he was sick on Monday, he would be unable to function for at least an entire week. During sixth grade he missed thirteen weeks of school.

All my training as a pediatrician was no help. No one seemed to be able to offer any insight; many seemed to imply that there was something drastically wrong with my parenting, that I wasn't firm enough The common advice of the time was to drag the child with a school phobia to school, come hell or high water. There was no way this tactic would work with my son. I really wanted to understand how Neal was feeling and I learned more about school phobia and childhood depression than I had during all my years of practice. I began to develop enormous compassion for the parents and patients with this problem.

This insoluble problem came to its crisis at the end of his eighth grade year when the Director of the Menlo School in Menlo Park, California where Neal was enrolled called me in for a consultation. She, who loved the school and valued its reputation, was terribly upset. "No one," she told me, "has ever before failed eighth grade at our school." But Neal had—mostly by absence but also by not doing assignments. For her, it was an unbelievable situation.

There was nothing I could do but find him another—perhaps more suitable—school and have another try. My boy was bright; he could excel, but the highly competitive atmosphere of private schools turned him off completely.

This story comes with a happy ending. By fall Neal was enrolled in a small public High School, James Lick in San José, and finding his place with school work and friends. During his first year he tried out for, and won the chance to become, the James Lick Comets mascot, joining the team cheerleaders in costume with a big round comet head. In his Senior year he was elected class president. Today Neal is a tall, well-adjusted adult who lives with friends. I see him frequently and he is always available to fix my computer or keep me company.

Radio West

Jocelyn Orr

"This is London!" And it was—6,000 miles away. Most likely these were the first radio words ever heard in my five-year-old life as I was scrambling around the small kitchen of the reporter's mother, Ethel Murrow. Seated at the table with Mrs. Murrow (which is what I always had to call her) were my mother and a few invited loggers.

Somehow word had arrived at the logging camp that, if our next door neighbors would drive the very curvy roads to the city of Port Angeles, Washington there was something called a "radio" to be picked up. It had been sent by their youngest son, Egbert Roscoe, later to be known as Edward R. Murrow, to hear him broadcast from Vienna as well as London. This promised to be a momentous event as we barely had electricity, only Pete Peterson's weak generator that was set to go off every night at 7:00 p.m. President Franklin D. Roosevelt, without Eleanor, had even stopped by on his way to dedicate Olympic National Park and to promise electricity. Rural electrification was an important part of his public program.

On that kitchen table was an awkward-looking wooden box. It held no interest for me since it was silent. Next to it, Roscoe Murrow, Ed's father, had laid out a pocket watch. At some specific second, not about to waste any battery time, he turned the radio on. The voice that came out was terrifying to me. I thought that someone had shoved Ed into a small box. How could he escape? But every Sunday we would troop over to hear his broadcast. Mrs. Murrow, a Quaker from the Carolinas, would look very worried at times and it finally dawned on me that she was concerned about his safety generally, rather than his being entrapped in a box. I vowed to myself that I would never visit this London wherever it was because it was always on fire. About ten years later I was privileged to see it for the first time during the "austerity" period. My father, who functioned as chief engineer and surveyor, was one of the few loggers of British descent—from Scotland and England.

Bloedel-Donovan, a Canadian-American logging company, was harvesting what seemed then was an endless expanse of Douglas fir at the northwest edge of the United States: the Olympic Peninsula of Washington state. Situated on a small prairie was a logging camp occupied by about 60 families in company cottages. Many of the loggers had been through World War I and the Depression. Many had married school-teachers, a civilizing experience. In nearby Forks, these teachers had founded the westernmost branch of the American Association of University Women. They took it upon themselves to improve the plight of the elementary school children living in the many nearby squalid Indian reservations, mostly Makah. The headquarters of the company, the town Sappho, also had a number of members of AAUW. Why should a strictly company town be named for a lesbian Greek goddess? Later that was puzzling to me. I never found an answer.

I liked Sappho because it had a company store. There were scarred wooden sidewalks above the mud, almost worn to splinters because of the loggers' spiked boots. It barely exists now as the buildings were all removed from their foundations and sent on barges to British Columba to be re-used.

Roscoe Murrow had a highly visible role in the camp as he was the only engineer of the Sappho locomotive which dragged out trees of a size never to be seen again. Living today, he would have been distressed by the puny trees being removed. That man always waved to us children as he drove his train through the logging camp. He could see us, but we weren't close by. We were never allowed to come near to the logging area where the danger was so great. And there were lots of those dangerous areas. Often Roscoe hauled explosives on the empty back of flat cars with "powder monkeys" (two men) huddled over the charges. "Powder monkeys" were expendable; the train engine was not. (When the bosses came inspecting, a caboose was added.)

These men worked in a "forest primeval," just the way the poet said it.

My Dad's job included laying out train routes and landings on special heavy wax paper to keep them from being washed away in the constant rain. He hated the rain slipping down his neck. He had to drag the surveyor's transits and axes, all kinds of gear, and make maps through the underbrush and the forest. There were bears and cougars and even bad brush—devil's club, for example, which grew to four-feet in height and five-feet wide. The man badly needed an assistant.

The Murrows had sent two boys through Washington State College (now a university) and couldn't afford to send Ed when it would have been his turn. He had to finance his own education and so he dropped out to earn the money for room and board. (The other two went on to have distinguished careers: Lt. General in World War II and Chief Engineer for the whole state of Washington.)

My Dad was allowed to hire Ed whom he thought was the finest young man he had ever met. Setting out for work, the two would don their "tin pants", waterproofs, and bright red hats, so poachers wouldn't mistake them for elk or moose. They would camp out together once they had penetrated the brush and forests. Later Ed would write my Dad about the "phony" barbecues he attended in the Hamptons of Long Island, New York. When he built a weekend house in the same state he included the monument marker by its front door. It was one which he and my father had both signed when they found a corner section through the transit.

At that time there was a national education foundation which sent every student body president of certain colleges and universities to New York City and then on to Europe. Ed had never been east of the Idaho panhandle, but he went and was elected president of the entire group to go. This was an unprecedented honor for someone from a college of which no Easterner had ever heard.

In the thirties, when Ed was already in Europe, CBS more or less drafted him. Logging's loss became broadcasting's gain. He traded in the red hat and tin pants for an English trench coat and snappy fedora.

In Bellingham, Washington we would visit the retired elder Murrows, for the first time in their own home, not one owned by the company. Ed would come out from his apartment in New York City to see his folks. His Dad had been felled by a stroke and sat speechless in a wheelchair. Ed would visit them a few times a year, charter an ocean fishing boat during the week, and then visit again. It was very much like him to prefer the wild Pacific, instead of the calmer waters of Puget Sound. I remember how excited he was after visiting Marshall Tito in Yugoslavia. I was excited, too, because I got an "A" on a University of Washington political science paper I wrote about Tito, analyzing him. Of course, it was all based on inside information.

The elder Murrows had the latest advances of radios and television in their home. At one point it looked as if their place had more antennae than the Bellingham police station. As a young person it was always fun to see my first color tv and the radios there. The Murrows said it was all donated by the local appliance dealer. We doubted it. What Ed had started with the miraculous radio so many years ago he kept up.

My father was finding the work in the forest becoming more difficult with age. Although he probably didn't make much money at the time, there wasn't anything to buy anyway. He had been investing his wages in a Tacoma, Washington plywood plant and it was time to leave the most remote area of the United States and go on to somewhere else, buying lumber, and selling plywood in a genuine city.

At one time early in our marriage, Jim, a physicist with a graduate degree, was stationed at a secret Signal Corps Camp out of Fort Monmouth, New Jersey. Ed invited the two of us for a personal tour of CBS. Unfortunately, we turned it down because the Senator Joseph McCarthy had investigated Camp Evans and he and Ed were engaged in broadcast warfare. (Ed won.) The Senator had even denounced him as belonging to the Communist Party (the IWW, Wobblies). It was fear of losing his top secret security clearance that dictated that refusal for Jim. Those who had known Ed as a logger signed a deposition for the Senate which exonerated him.

Throughout my professional life I was comfortable with distinguished scientists and celebrities. I worked five years for the U. S. Geological Survey and two years for double Noble scholar, Linus Pauling, in a social and fund-raiding capacity. In the course of his life Ed moved from wild, rural America to sophisticated, modern cities, interviewing both rogues and rulers. What did we have in common? A deep reverence for nature and a thoroughly American background.

Da Ultimate Yoke (The Ultimate Joke)

Joanne Szybalski

Da Ultimate Yoke
Is God's yoke on us, a cosmic yoke.

Ve tink ve are so important.
Ve spend our lives
Trying to be perfect.
Until finally
Vone day God says
Vel, that's all over,
And it is…

A great yoke on us!
Dat's it.
No second chance.
You had your turn…
Next?

Vat to do wid dis sad situation?
Dere might be some rules to follow.
Rule vone: Talk to God along da vay.
Rule two: Make every recevest
Fight its vay to stay

On da priority ladder.
Rule tree: Fight, fight, fight for Vashington State
(or vatever your school is).
You've got to get your yuices flowing!

Get in da game,
Because, at any moment,
God may appear
Vit da message:
Times Up!

Summers with Gagi

Bill Friedrichs

When I was a small tot I couldn't say "Grandma." Instead, the word "Gagi" ("Gah-gi") came out. I was the oldest of the cousins and they followed my choice so the name Gagi stuck. It became adopted by our elders as well, and eventually everyone in the family called my Grandmother by the same name.

From the time I was eight years old until I was 12, I spent two weeks out of every summer with Gagi at her cabin in Hopland, a small town in northern California. Of course, it was primitive, but I loved it. I always associated summer with California's golden hills which were dotted with majestic dark oak trees. As a young boy, I counted the days 'til we went to the country. What a change it was from my life in San Francisco!

The town of Hopland was only two blocks long, but our daily trips included stops at the Post Office and General Store. As we left the main highway from town headed toward the cabin, we took a dirt road which had several gated cattle guards along the way. My job then was to open and close them all.

Gagi knew the man who farmed near her cabin and stopped to visit while I played in the barn jumping into the haystacks and, outside, swinging on a homemade tire swing. While we were there, we bought fresh eggs and milk that had been taken from the cow that day.

My Grandmother was an independent woman and a no-nonsense type. When she had just bought a new car, she enjoyed driving her own shiny black Chevy Coupe. She was a husky woman with white hair and glasses who seemed to enjoy my company on our trips.

Going to the cabin was a real adventure for me. I could play in the creek, read comic books, eat orange ice cream icicles, and see all the farm animals when Gagi visited her friends at their homes. During those years there was a time when I would pretend to be Tarzan and jump from rock to rock in the river. I would even swing on the tree vines over the bushes below, yelling like him all the while. It was a great time and place for a preteen youngster!

Gagi's cabin was rustic and consisted of one big room plus a kitchen and bath. There was a loft over the living room. That was where Gagi slept. Some nights her snoring was so loud I had a hard time sleeping. I would yell, "Gagi, you're snoring!" but she never seemed to hear me.

Before we went to bed at night we would play cards and read by the light of a kerosene lamp and I would chronicle our activities by writing to my folks.

During the day my chores included filling water pails from the creek and bringing them back to her cabin. I would dip a ladle into the clear, cool water and enjoy a refreshing drink.

There was a path from behind the cabin that led past the outhouse and along the creek. It eventually came to a swimming hole. I dubbed this place the "Big Hole." I used to love to visit the Big Hole and would use my arms and kick my legs hoping one day I would learn to swim. Watching from the side of the water, Gagi would shout words of encouragement.

"Kick your legs, Billy! You can do it!"

I thought I never would, but one day I made it all the way across. I knew then that I had conquered my fears about not being able to swim. I practiced the backstroke, the crawl, and the breaststroke and was quite proud of my accomplishments.

Years later I went back to see the Big Hole and was surprised and somewhat disappointed at how small it was and what a short distance it was from one side to the other.

Gagi had a kind of rock garden. One day she was working there in her garden putting in some plants when I heard her give a yell. I raced over and found that she had disturbed a rattlesnake from its lair. She quickly picked up her rake to hold the snake down and yelled for me to grab the long-handled hatchet. While she held the snake down just behind the head, I chopped it off in one stroke. For years afterwards she would tell the story about how "Brave little Billy saved my life!"

In fact, it was a shared triumph.

Two Trips Around the World:
A Wanderer's Story

Jim White

In the summer of 1958, when I was 28, I decided that I would like to travel to Europe. Along with earning my Master's in Business Administration at the University of Michigan, I had audited classes in music and art appreciation and wanted to experience what I had studied first-hand. I had saved $2,500 while working at Sutherland Paper Company and found a 90-day tour of major European capitals I could afford. When I heard about the Youth Hostel Program where I could get a good meal for $1 and could stay a night for $1.25, I decided to travel on my own and see how long my money would last. What had begun as a summer vacation became a two-and-a-half year adventure that expanded my horizons and enhanced my life in many ways.

My first stop was Montreal where I boarded a ship on the Europe Canada Line, the SS *Seven Seas*. I was amazed to discover that it took two and one-half days to get down the St. Lawrence River to the open ocean. We went on across the Atlantic to Portsmouth, Le Havre, and Rotterdam where I got off and took rooms for a couple of nights. My hotel was on the edge of the red light district. I was interested in meeting local people and learning about them so I took the opportunity to talk with some of the girls on the street there. They'd chat with me for a bit until a paying customer came along and then they'd move on.

From Rotterdam I decided to explore the British Isles because my father had always said that he was a mix of English, Irish, Scotch, and Dutch. I took deck passage on a ferry to Great Yarmouth and Norwich in a pouring rain. We were huddled on benches under a tarp overhang when I heard a woman say, "Ow abow ta cupper, luv?" I wasn't yet accustomed to British English and didn't even realize that she was talking to me until the fellow behind me said, "She's asking if you want some tea." I was very grateful for the hot tea and "biscuits" (cookies) she was offering. She couldn't figure out where I came from because I didn't have an eastern or southern American accent, but she encouraged me to keep talking because she enjoyed hearing me. Another man I met on the ferry learned that I was possibly interested in teaching and suggested that I visit his friend, a schoolmaster in Denmark, to see the school. I decided to go there after I left the British Isles.

From London, with an American flag on my rucksack, I hitchhiked to Wales, then to Ireland—Dublin and Belfast—and stayed a week in a hostel in Kilarney. I took a walk around the lake and was surprised to find it was 25 miles and took me 10 hours to walk around. Scotland was next. I planned to walk around Loch Ness, but after refusing several rides I finally accepted one from a persistent driver. Hitchhiking in Europe at that time was very easy with plenty of rides available. As I traveled, I found that gas stations were excellent places to find rides. I went as far north as Aberdeen in Scotland and then headed south.

After returning to Rotterdam, I found a ride to Hamburg and then hitchhiked to Odense, Denmark. From there I walked the last two miles to Seden where I met the schoolmaster, Svend, his wife Lisa, and their daughters. I stayed for several days, visiting the school and meeting the children as they studied where I was from on their maps. While I enjoyed seeing the school, the best part of the visit was getting to know the family and experiencing Danish life first-hand. I have remained friends with them and, even now 55 years later, still visit with the daughters and their families.

Then on to Copenhagen where the youth hostels were all full. I ended up sharing an apartment with three other youth hostellers and together we learned many ways to save money. We rented a room over a bakery and got fresh pastries each morning for breakfast at a reduced price. The Carlsburg and Tuborg Brewery tours offered free bratwurst, crackers, and cheese in their tasting rooms. I visited the Tivoli Gardens and took advantage of the free admission to the museums. That was when I learned that the first thing I should do in each new city was get the museum card for student admission prices to all the museums. In each major city I visited I stayed until I felt I had seen all I could and then I moved on.

Norway was next—a youth hostel in Oslo. The only thing served for breakfast in the hostel was brown cheese. I didn't think I would like the cheese but, with no other choice, I tried it and discovered it tasted great. I even took a few slices along with bread to have for my lunches. The Vigeland Museum and Sculpture Park were especially interesting to me and I visited several times. I took a boat down the Sonia Fjord to the youth hostel at its end. Every day I went for a quick (very cold) swim in the fjord and hiked in the mountains. After I left, a week later, I realized that I had left my watch behind and then I discovered something great about the country: my watch was still there, being saved for me to pick up! That wouldn't have been the same in Italy.

Next I moved on to Stockholm, Sweden, where I found a youth hostel on a sailing schooner, the SS *Chapman*. We had to be in before 10 o'clock or we'd be locked out. The woman running the hostel suggested I go to the opera and, when I protested that I couldn't afford it, she told me about standing room. I saw *Die Fledermaus* for $1.50. I enjoyed it so much that I went back again the next night!

Then it was back to hitchhiking to visit a college friend, George Bleekman, who was teaching at Pattonville Army Base near Stuttgart. I guess for the sake of supporting the local economy there were laws there against hosting visitors. But finding shelter was easy: I slept in an Army base storage locker in an attic for a couple of weeks until the security guard caught me.

Before leaving Pattonvllle I bought a used VW bug for $400. (I sold it later for $325.) Then I drove south though Yugoslavia. At one pension I was served a huge platter of chops with my eggs—a memorable breakfast! Plumbing, I have to say, was very rudimentary. My main entertainment in most of the towns where I stopped along the way was spending the evening in the main square where the local people would gather to walk around, talking together.

From Yugoslavia I drove into Greece and found a hostel on the edge of Athens where I had to do 40 pushups to get in. Once accepted, I played chess most days with the man in charge, the man who wouldn't allow anyone in who wasn't fit to stay. I was there for two weeks and didn't drive anywhere during that time because it wasn't considered safe to leave a car unattended in central Athens. Instead, I used the inexpensive buses and trolleys to see all the famous buildings and museums. Then it was back through Yugoslavia and into Italy where I made the mistake of driving on a beach. The tide was coming in and my car got stuck. I went to find a wrecker, but by the time I got back a guy on the beach had found a plank to lever the car up enough to be safe back on solid ground. I took it to a garage to get it dried out and then went south through Rome and as far as Naples and Capri.

I stayed in the men's dorm in a youth hostel in Rome where I joined some men who were making their dinner by spreading butter on a slice of bread they had bought at a bakery. They had bigger plans for eating, however. When night fell, knowing that I wasn't going to go with them, they handed me a length of rope and told me to tie it to the post of my double-decker bed. They were counting on me to help them get in and out of the window when they went foraging. I think they must have known what they were doing because they came back loaded up with carrots, potatoes, and cabbages—all sorts of vegetables—to supplement their meager diet.

After Italy I continued west across the French Riviera to Barcelona, Spain. I made a quick detour to Andorra where there was a good exchange rate for dollars. The customs officials seemed to be looking for smugglers because they went through my whole car, opening suitcases, sifting dirt in my hubcaps, even removing the back seat from my car. They left me to put it all back together. I continued west to southern Spain to the western border town of Badojoz where I left the car in a square feeling it would be safest there and took a train to Lisbon for two days and a bus back. My car was safely waiting for me when I returned. I headed back across Spain to Madrid. There were many checkpoints along the roads in that country where soldiers with automatic weapons were checking up on local people traveling on the major highways. They had no interest in tourists, however, so I had no problems.

While in Spain I had met an Austrian who said if I ever got to St. Anton he had a pair of old skis he would sell me for $10. When I was in Austria, I went to St. Anton, bought the skis, and stayed for six weeks while I learned to ski. Those skis didn't have bindings, just straps to hold them on, but I was able to master the basics with them and enjoyed skiing for many years.

Still driving, I went back to Seden, Denmark, picking up three men on the way. When the generator on the car went out, the German, Pete Munks from Dusseldorf, read the German manual for my car. (His father was a survivor of Stalingrad and later I had interesting conversations with him.) The Belgian was a good mechanic and the Australian, Tony Carr, from Bear's Lagoon, a sheep station near Bendigo, Australia, jacked up my car. Together they repaired it and we continued on our way. When Tony Carr left, he said, "You bloody bugger, if you ever want to see a great country, come and see us in Australia." I took him up on the offer, but not until I had finished my travels in Europe.

After a good visit with my new friends in Seden and a return visit to Stockholm, I drove through the Soviet Zone to West Berlin. I hadn't been able to find anyone in the hostels willing to drive to Berlin, but I was determined to see it and went alone. I stayed on the main highway and had no problems. I was even able to drive into East Berlin through Checkpoint Charlie to see the Berlin Opera performance of *Madame Butterfly*, my first opera in a major Opera House. I was enthralled—the music was overwhelming—and my lifelong love of opera was born.

Stopping by Pattonville again, I was able to sell the VW and, with $600 left, I headed to England. I found that was enough for a ticket on a P & O ship to Australia. In October of 1959 I took the HMS *Strathnaver* around Spain with a stop at Gibraltar, on into the Mediterranean, through the Suez Canal, to Port Said to Bombay, India, and on to Ceylon and across the Indian Ocean. Air temperature was well over 100 degrees. My room was right over the Engine Room and the floor was so hot that I couldn't walk on it barefoot. I slept in the Veranda Café on the daytime lounges after everyone else had gone back to their cabins.

A dentist and his family I met on the ship told me that it was foolish not to get off and see the places where the ship stopped weekly. I hadn't known that I could get off at any port and catch the next P & O ship to continue my trip. I took his advice, got off at Perth, and stayed with him and his family for a week. The next stop I made was at Adelaide where I stayed with a teacher who took me all around, showing me the Barossa Valley and the wines being produced there.

It was then on to Melbourne where Tony Carr met me. The family had an apartment there and, after some sightseeing, Tony drove me to Bendigo and on to Bear's Lagoon Sheep Station where I stayed for six months. The station had 12,000 acres with 3,000 head of cattle, and 10-12,000 Merino sheep, all free range. The rams could take care of themselves. They were really robust and hard to hold. (I learned very quickly that, with my long legs, I couldn't hold them well enough to learn to shear them.) There were water tanks around the outback range for the sheep and, besides the livestock, many acres of wheat being grown.

Those six months were full of "adventures" that I took part in. Perhaps the most dramatic was the burning of the sheep. One morning I was told to put on my oldest clothes. Then I watched the tractors drag wood into an enormous pile before we set it on fire. Given a long-handled shovel, I was told to use it. I soon saw how. The others were bringing in diseased or other dead sheep and throwing them on the wood pile. As 60-70 sheep were added, part of my job was to see that they went right into the flames and stayed there. Another part was to control the run-off of the liquid debris from their remains, to shovel it back in. When the burning was over, I took a truck home and was told by the woman of the house, "Stop! Stop right here and take off all your clothing. NOW! I've seen grown men naked before!" Filthy and smelly, I had to shower outdoors, too, before I went in. All my clothes were burned.

During the night shift I drove a tractor pulling a 20-foot seeder to re-seed 2,000 acres of wheat that had died during the drought. I put in fence posts, too. Tony remarked, "I finally found something you're good for." He said that because, at 6' 4" to his 5' 6", I could reach the top of the wood posts and work the hand driver to pound them into the ground. On horseback, I learned to move sheep all day through stiles and gates, waiting each time until the lead one decided to go through. At first I rode in my hiking boots and, one day, the horse's halter broke and she ran away. I couldn't get my boots out of the stirrups to jump off so had to stay put until she stopped just in front of a barbed wire fence. After that I wore my tennis shoes when riding.

The family dog got distemper from some of the other dogs on the station and, because no one in the family could bear to do it, I was asked to be the executioner. I put him in a bag, walked him off a ways, and used a shotgun.

The pubs were so crowded at the four p.m. "Swill on Sundays" that there was only space to put a glass down where its automatic refill, when the liquid had gotten down to one inch remaining, was marked on a coaster. I could only manage two or three marks, but some guys had 20-25 marks on their coasters.

With Tony and his brother, Peter, I drove to a neighboring farm where I nursed one scotch all night and danced with the neighbor's wife while the Carr boys drank beer with the farmer. I was the one who had to drive the MG home with one of the Carrs each draped over a fender. They were throwing up but, just the same, exulting that they had drunk the other guy under the table. What I learned was that Aussies work hard and play hard. They drank 30 quarts of Victorian Export Beer (12%) that evening.

After I left the sheep station I still wanted to see more of Australia, so I went up the east coast to Heron Island and the Great Barrier Reef for a week. Then I wanted to go across the top of the continent to Darwin. I was warned to take a transport to assure getting all the way and not being stranded in the middle of nowhere, but I couldn't get any of them to stop and pick me up. When I mentioned that I would walk along the road at night, people warned me that snakes come out on the warm road at night and that Australia is full of poisonous snakes. I dropped the idea. I got as far as Rockhampton and, after spending a night in the little bit of shelter offered by the doorjamb of the entryway of a school in pouring rain, I turned back and hitched a ride with a truck driver headed for Sydney. As it turned out, he drove too fast and on the wrong side of the road which made this the scariest time of the whole trip. I left as soon as he stopped for gas.

Once I was safely in Sydney I needed a job to earn enough money to get home. The paper advertised a room in a boarding house, Ma Grill's, and I took it. I went out every day to look for a job in the financial area where I could use my brokerage experience. While on the ship, I had learned of an American, Ian MacFarland, who was a partner in a small investment management company, Charles Ord and Minette. I interviewed with him and had a job after only one week, writing up reports on companies and changing currency figures from short Australian pounds into long English pounds and dollars. One very good company studied was Broken Hill Propriety (now known as BHP Billiton Limited) which mined iron ore. I sent reports to England and the United States to get buyers.

Immigration had told me that I really shouldn't be working since I didn't have a work visa, but they sent me the necessary paperwork so I could keep my job. I paid five pounds a week for room and board and earned eight or nine pounds a week plus overtime. I could sometimes make 15 pounds a week. I worked in Sydney for six months and, while I was there, I went surfing with a Brit. We got caught in a rip tide and had to let it take us out at least half a mile. Then we were able to swim way around to get to shore. I learned not to fight a rip tide, but to let it take you until it eases. We made it to shore 90 minutes later.

The only letter my father ever wrote to me was sent to Sydney saying, "It's about time you came home." So I bought a ticket and started off through Singapore and Manila. In Hong Kong I bought two suits and a cashmere overcoat which were delivered to the ship two days later. I wore them for many years; my son still has the overcoat. The ship continued on to Japan where I climbed Mt. Fuji and stayed in a Tokyo youth hostel. I remember pushers who squeezed everyone into the subway and snail soup, rice, and raw egg for breakfast.

I left Japan for Hawaii, then on to Long Beach, California where I started to hitchhike back to Michigan. Once I got as far as Denver I found I could get a drive-away car to take to Seattle. I changed directions and, after delivering the car, went to my sister's apple ranch in Wenatchee in eastern Washington. I worked there sorting in the shed and picking apples long enough to get enough money to get back to Ann Arbor. Once there, I took some jobs I didn't enjoy, but I had the good luck to bump into a person from Sutherland Paper Company who said I should give them a try again since I was already trained. They hired me. Sent to Texas to work in Dallas and Houston, I lasted one year. By that time I had saved enough money to travel again.

In the winter of 1962-3, I went to Europe to ski for two weeks and came back two years later. I was retracing some old steps but new things happened along the way. In Switzerland I met a woman who was clearing out her liquor cupboard. I ended up with a rucksack full of fifths of various liquors so heavy that I took the train to Denmark to move it all. Where I sat, I could hear the bottles gurgling in the rucksack in the corridor. I didn't declare the alcohol at the border because I knew I couldn't afford the tariff. I had the risk of its being taken, but I got through all right. When I arrived, I offered my friend Svend his choice. He took a fifth of crème de menthe; he and his buddy drank the whole bottle that evening. I used the remaining bottles as gifts when I stayed with other people on my travels.

A coastal steamer carried me along the Yugoslavian Dalmatian Coast, then on to Greece. From there, I was able to catch a boat to Chios where I had heard there was a daily boat to the mainland. As it turned out, I was the only passenger who needed a ride that day. Once on the mainland I took the bus to Istanbul, enjoyed the area, and then took the train back to Yugoslavia. I took the Italian liner, SS *Saturnia,* from Trieste to Spain where I began hitchhiking again. After standing all day in the rain waiting for a ride in southern Spain, I went to the train station and found out that I could take a train all the way to Denmark for only $45.00. I visited my Danish family friends again and every day took their dog on a walk while I rode a bike. They still joke that each time I ended up bringing him home on the handlebars.

Next stop: London where in March of 1964 I left on the HMS *Orsova*, a P & O ship bound for Australia. Reaching Melbourne, I stayed at Tony Carr's apartment in town for four weeks and did yard work between sightseeing jaunts while I was there. I didn't go back to the sheep station.

I continued on to Japan, and when I was talking to a woman on our ship there, I mentioned that I had climbed Mt. Fuji. Even though she was very overweight and middle-aged, she was determined to climb it herself and begged me to take her. After I refused several times, I decided that I would do it and we started off at four a.m. up a scree slope, that is, two steps forward up and then slide one step back, back and forth, back and forth. After the first hour of doing that, she hired two boys who had a rope. They took turns pushing and pulling her. At every station along the way she stopped for a needed 15-minute rest and to get brands burned on her walking stick. She insisted that I have the burns done, too, to prove what we had done. I stayed with her to the top, all the four-to-five hours before she finally made it. Then I left her and ran down in 30 minutes.

Going home across the Pacific was pretty dramatic. We ran into the backside of a typhoon for a couple of days. The big waves were 50- to 70-feet high, washing onto the highest deck with a railing, just below the top recreation deck. Some 90% of the passengers never left their cabins; some even got themselves tied into their bunks. A few of those who tried to move around ended up with fractured arms and other injuries. I never missed a meal myself, but a lot of it was bread, crackers, hot tea, and soup. I moved very cautiously holding on to railings. We docked in Vancouver, Canada and I headed back to Ann Arbor.

I thoroughly enjoyed all the sights I saw on my travels, but the most enduring part has been all I gained from the many experiences I shared with numerous people from around the world.

Enrolled in the University of Michigan again, I earned a teaching credential and headed west to see where I could find a teaching job. I ended up in Tacoma, Washington at Lincoln High School where I taught business subjects and became the Swimming Coach. Fourteen years later I moved to Stadium High School, teaching another 16 years before retiring in 1995. I remained in Tacoma painting houses and doing odd jobs until I retired to another kind of life at the Saratoga Retirement Community.

A Singer's Tale

June Clodius

In the middle of the Depression I was born to a loving Christian family: Dad, Mom, and sister, Charlotte. The location was Englewood, Colorado, a small suburb of Denver. My childhood was a happy time and we were fortunate as my Dad had a steady job at the Gates Rubber Company. However, since his salary was only $16 a week, we always had a big vegetable garden, raised chickens, and Dad helped at Grandpa's sugar beet farm on Saturdays to bring home good beef for special occasions.

My mother was a great musician. She taught piano and always served as a church organist. I was encouraged to sing when very young and, during my high schooling, my parents sacrificed to give me voice lessons. My interest was to study at the famous Julliard School and my teacher was working to find a scholarship so I might continue my vocal training there. After a short time at Colorado University I returned to Denver to study and prepare for further vocal training at night. During the day I worked for a doctor. (I also sang at a funeral home, hiding my white uniform behind a curtain.) As it happened, a young Denver University student in the church choir turned my head and we were married. Julliard was out of the picture then. Carl, my husband, encouraged my vocal career so I enjoyed many years of soloing in my church and other special performances such as light opera.

New direction came with my music career of soloing and performing. I was also raising two children and encouraging Carl as he pursued a Pupil Personnel Credential at Stanford University.

Then a big change came to our family: we moved to San José, California in the fall of 1963. Carl became a high school counselor; I cared for the family and continued to sing in the Bay area—propelled by my ambitious vocal teacher.

Life has had many health challenges for me. At 45 years of age I was diagnosed with cancer. After my left mastectomy and radiation, two years of chemotherapy followed. The fear that came upon me was of dying. How would it come about? How could I leave my family behind? Then I recalled my Grandmother's two words: "BUT GOD." What she always meant by those words was "But God will get me through!" She had become a widow at 21 years of age and already had a little one-year-old girl (my mother.) Life was tough for Grandma, but her spirit was always trusting and positive, knowing God was there. Her words were meaningful for me.

With remission Carl and I enjoyed traveling in Europe, attending several Elderhostel programs, plus some cruises. Then, 14 years later, it was suspected that the cancer had invaded my lung. I had lung surgery but, fortunately, no cancer was there.

During the following year I had my second bout with cancer and another mastectomy. Many times I cried, "Enough, God! Enough!" Our two children were grown, in college, and working. Again I said, "BUT GOD," and He truly brought me through.

Sixteen years ago, after 47 plus years of marriage, my loving husband and caretaker, Carl, died. Yes, life has been difficult with lots of changes. After saying "NEVER! NEVER!" for over seven years and another "But God!", I had decided never to marry again. I wanted to protect myself from further loss and heartbreak. But something happened that changed my mind. A friend was helping me with the computer he had sold me and I had invited him to dine at a restaurant to thank him for his help. He had lost his wife, my dear friend, Rita, with whom our families had been close for years. To my surprise, the restaurant was closed, so he, Jerry, announced that this meal was to be his treat. He took me to another restaurant. We reminisced and enjoyed a delicious meal. As we chatted, he asked if it would be all right to ask my son, Kevin, if he could court me.

We both knew the end point of courting: marriage. I asked him not to question Kevin because I was of an age to make my own decisions and, besides, we had been good friends—like brother and sister—for 40 years. I would NEVER marry again.

But something happened to change my mind.

I had become interested in watching "***Doctor Phil***" on the television and one night I was especially impressed with his kind and knowledgeable answer to a participant who, like me, couldn't seem to get over the loss of a loved one. The doctor told the man, "Imagine yourself sitting in the back seat of a car looking out the rear window. There is a beautiful world to see out the front, but you are missing it all." The words that I heard were like lightning to me. *I* was the one looking out the back window as I traveled down the road with beautiful scenery ahead. *I* was the one missing something wonderful. These words gave me great hope that I could move on and anticipate the beautiful life ahead with Jerry.

Jerry says, "God flang us together." We were married in the beautiful redwoods at Mount Hermon Christian Conference Center nine months later on September 26, 2004. Our children walked the aisle with us and "gave us away."

Jerry has been a wonderful caretaker. We had been married only a short time when I had open-heart surgery and then a reoccurrence of cancer.

Life has often been difficult but we take each day as it comes. We are so enjoying our lives together and anticipate more time to travel and enjoy family. As we celebrate our ninth anniversary in the fall we look forward to many wonderful years here at the Saratoga Retirement Community—to each new activity and each new friend.

A Niagara Experience

Isik Doluca

Coming from Turkey, we arrived in New York City on May 28th of 1963. It was a very hot and humid day. There were four of us—my husband, our two sons, and me. This was one of my husband's business trips which he used to take a lot for his work. He disappeared for two or three months and several times even for four months. I never joined him on these trips because I didn't want to be under his feet.

One day he said that he had to go to New York City for two months. This time I said, "I'm joining you with our two sons!"

It seems that it was a very good decision because we stayed there for two years instead of two months! We rented a furnished apartment in Flushing, Long Island. There we were close to a couple, our friends from Turkey. On the first morning of our arrival we woke up to a terrible noise! The building was shaking! We were right next to the Long Island railway. But it didn't take long to get used to that noise the way you get used to anything in life.

We stayed in that apartment for only one year. One day our landlord called us and told us that he was getting married. They were planning to move in and we had to move out. It was very difficult to find a furnished place because we had two sons, six and three years old. Most renters didn't know how well behaved our two sons were!

Kutlu, my husband, came home with the good news that he had found an apartment in Manhattan on a block next to the Hudson River. The landlady was very happy to rent it since they had two sons almost the same ages as ours. The location of this new place was much more convenient because the Engineering

Company's office was in Manhattan. We always used the subway since we didn't own a car.

We had a wonderful one year in that apartment. A model, beautiful, young lady lived upstairs. She was a Protestant; another family lived across from us with one girl the same age as our older son. That family was Catholic. The landlady, who lived on the first floor, was Jewish. And we had moved there from a Moslem country. What a wonderful mixture we were! The ladies came to our small hall with their children to have tea. All of us enjoyed every minute of it every afternoon.

We used to go to museums, concerts, and ballet shows in the city. A few times we took our neighbors with us to Carnegie Hall, the Metropolitan Opera, and Lincoln Center. Some of them used to say, "We were born in New York and have lived here all our lives, but we have never been to such places. Here comes a couple from Turkey and they take us to these places!"

There were 52 sightseeing locations on the subway map. In two years we went to all of them by subway. One time we wanted to go to the Niagara Falls. Our Turkish friends in Flushing, who hadn't been there before either, had a car. Another Turkish couple decided to join us so we went in two cars.

The falls were magnificent. It was a beautiful day. We were admiring everything: the water, the falls, and the scenery all around it. All of a sudden I couldn't see our younger son, Sinan, my three-year-old anywhere. All of us—Kutlu, my older son Tunc who was six-years-old, all our friends—started looking around. I was crying. (Mothers always think of the worst things first. I was thinking maybe he had fallen down the falls and drowned!) Kutlu, Tunc, and I were cuddling each other and crying. People all around us were asking why we were crying. All of them, including our friends, were looking around to find the little boy.

For about an hour everybody was searching everywhere to find him. Then somebody came running towards us, saying a lady was holding a little boy in her arms. He was crying. At last we saw the woman holding our son. She was asking him questions, but he didn't know a word of English! He was only crying very hard. When he saw us, he jumped into my lap and we hugged each other. Then all four of us were hugging each other and crying with relief for a long time. Everyone who helped us was relieved, too.

I will always remember that terrible day at the Niagara Falls.

Later on during the same day we took a boat trip under the falls. This time we were very happy and we realized how much we loved each other. Our older son was so very happy to find his brother. I remember that, when the younger one was born, Tunc never got jealous of his brother. In those days the doctors recommended not holding babies on our laps to put them to sleep. They said that they should be in their own cribs and learn how to fall asleep by themselves. Under those conditions naturally they cry a long time. Our older son used to go to Sinan's crib and try to talk to him, to tell him his own stories, and put him to sleep. He was always successful.

When we used to go to seaside camps in the summer, Sinan always followed his older brother wherever he went. Every day they played together. People in the camps used to call Sinan "the shadow of Tunc." We were lucky parents to have two very good-natured sons.

Years later, they built their homes on a *cul-de-sac* across from each other in Saratoga.

Notes on Being an Actress

Esther Wedner

I have never thought of myself in those terms—being an actress. I was, as a child, recognized by my teachers as an excellent reader because I always read words in complete sentences with the feelings that I thought they meant and deserved. To my mind, words are not merely letters on paper or the web but need to be taken in context with other words. Just as *"No man is an island,"* neither does any word stand by itself. Words come alive for me, springing from the page.

Consequently, when there was a script to be shared with an audience either in my public school or the temple one which I attended four afternoons a week, I was always chosen to enact the female. An older Hebrew school student wrote scripts relevant to religious holidays. During the *Oneg Shabbat (in honor of the Sabbat)* after the service, we performed while others drank tea and nibbled cookies. I was often chosen to perform in these scripts. Oh, how I loved doing them!

Getting to the temple from home was not simple because I had to walk at least a mile each way. Nevertheless, I not only attended this temple on Friday evenings, but also for Saturday morning services, and Sunday school. When other friends were going to the Saturday afternoon movies, I was going from the temple to the public library.

As an adult, three days after I graduated from Tulane University I got married. From then on, I was busy being a wife and mother, eventually going back to school to obtain Elementary School Certification, and undertaking ten years of public school teaching. By then, I was already beginning to think about becoming a School Counselor. When I had made up my mind, I earned a Master's in Counseling

Education and began to work in a hospital School of Nursing. For 13 years I taught Communications and counseled student nurses there.

During that time span of professional and private life, an associate urged me to audition for a local production of the musical **Mame.** I liked the idea very much. When I decided to try out, I bought the recording and learned the music ahead of time. I got the title role and what fun it all turned out to be!

But sometimes things happen. It was during a performance of that extremely physical role that I sprained my back. Oh, suddenly what pain I felt! What a misfortune for a performer! But, as they say in the theater, "The show must go on!" and on I went. That night I sang my part but I couldn't dance. Somebody else had to do that for me. It was the last night of our weeklong run when, after the curtain went down, I heard someone asking me if I were going to the cast party. Of course, I had to go. It was when they brought out the beautifully decorated cake and sang "*Mame*" to me that I broke down in pain. My fellow partyers called an ambulance and I was carried off to the hospital where I stayed in traction for several days. You might say that I suffered for my art!

{In fact, that wasn't the only time I suffered for my art. When I was the mother in **Rashomon** kneeling before the Emperor pleading for the life of my daughter, I tore the meniscus in my knee and, as a result, had to have orthoscopic surgery on it.)

There were other performances I remember from my amateur career. One was **Father Knows Best** in which I was the main female character. I also played Yenta in two different productions of **Fiddler on the Roof** and Big Mama in **Cat on a Hot Tin Roof.** My sister once commented, "How could you remember all those lines?" Those were the days! It was easy.

My favorite activity is playacting or playreading. In my next life, I want to be an actress.

Now all my playacting is done sitting in a chair. But it's still fun…

Travels with Sally and Lee Ann

Sally Ravel and Lee Ann Wolfe

We had been close friends for many years, sharing child-raising, vacations, barbeques, and long conversations. When our own children were settled into colleges and early careers, both of us found our discussions often mentioned concerns about our elderly parents and relatives. We talked about the need to explore what options were open to our own families and other older folks.

We decided to embark on a tour and begin the investigation of all types of senior housing. What was available in the San Francisco Bay area and how did these communities differ from each other? Unable to find any accurate guide to what existed in our local area, we decided to research the various options that were open to seniors. Our copious notes enabled us to discuss the diverse programs and types of housing that were offered.

We talked about our interest in this issue to friends and family and began getting inquiries asking for information about what we had learned. Often those who wanted to know more about what options were out there declared, enthusiastically, that we ought to write a book. That must have been the spark that ignited our interest into action. When we told our husbands about our growing plans, they too were encouraging, giving us the confidence we needed to go forward. Without total understanding of the issues we were exploring, we ventured into the expanse of the Bay Area. We decided our interviews would cover staff, residents, amenities, and, of course, our own impressions. We were gathering lots of good material, but we still needed to find a publisher who would be as enthusiastic as we were about offering this information to older folks and their families.

While we were sure our queries to publishers would be overwhelmingly popular, that didn't turn out to be so. We could only guess that the young employees of these firms were not at all interested in the mature adult market. In time, we finally got a positive reply from a publisher in New York City. Since I, Sally, was about to visit my son who lived in the city, I was able to meet with his representative. Over a glass of wine I chatted about the usefulness of our information and how badly it was needed. The listener liked my presentation, gave me a sizable advance check, and requested our first completed section of the book. Unfortunately, our elation and impetus for working faster were diminished when he sent us a cancellation notice. To our delight he never asked for a refund. So while we continued our research in the Bay area, visiting various senior residences and communities, we still did not have a publisher.

Finally a local Berkeley editor responded to our book summary and told us she was enthused about its contents. She agreed that the information we offered was very useful to individuals, couples, and their concerned family members. Finally, the parameters for our first book were established. Off we went, traveling throughout the San Francisco Bay area, Monterey, Carmel, Napa Valley and all the way into the Sacramento region.

Our plan of attack consisted of making appointments with the administration of each place we visited. For the most part, we approached this with utmost honesty but, when pushed, we would modestly indicate that we were looking to find a suitable place for our parents or close friends. That always opened the door. We enjoyed many overnight invitations, lunches, and one-to-one visits with residents, almost always accompanied with a few laughs or even shared tears from touching moments.

Retirement Living, A Guide to the Best Residences in Northern California was an easy-to-read reference book that described the different types of housing which included Planned Adult Communities, Life Care, and Continuing Care retirement communities. Our book targeted mature folks in good health or with minor problems. What we wanted was to be a resource for seniors looking to make a retirement living move by choice, not out of desperation. Book signings, radio, and TV interviews followed—experiences that we both enjoyed.

Soon after our first book was published, we added Southern California and, in time, we expanded our books further to include the entire West Coast, with some parts of Oregon, and Washington. Our third book was titled *Retirement Living, a Guide to the Best Residences in California and the West.* It was published by, of all people, *The San José Mercury-News.* In our interview with them we had given a huge sales pitch, one that didn't relent for a minute. By the time we left, we had gotten them to commit to a directory that was beyond our wildest dreams. The fact that this was the first book they ever published was incidental to the amount of advertising they gave it.

Certainly all the libraries bought it and we don't recall how many copies were ordered by phone or mail. We initiated our thrust into what, for us, was a bold adventure with a two-pronged attack: one, find a publisher, and two, start an expanded research project directed toward retirement living facilities. We were primarily interested in Independent Retirement Living and only covered Skilled Nursing Facilities or Assisted Living if they were associated with Continuing or Life Care facilities. We wanted to be a resource for seniors looking to make a retirement living move by choice, not out of desperation.

Our series of retirement living works was widely utilized and, to this day, we still receive praise and inquires from people, as well as their children, who have used the books.

Some of the memorable highlights of our data collection follow:

While visiting a lovely retirement community in Napa Valley, a demure, proper, elderly lady remarked, ""I'm so glad you girls are writing this book. It was really a bitch finding this place!"

While in Pacific Grove, a charming resident insisted that we visit her apartment which had a gorgeous view of Monterey Bay. When we entered, this spry, elderly woman hopped on her stationery bicycle and proceeded to tell us the loving story of her marriage and the importance of keeping fit. The remark that followed has stayed with us both all these years: "Next to marrying my husband, moving here was the best decision I've ever made in my lifetime!"

The visit to a retirement living community in Hemet, California was overwhelmingly the funniest experience we had. To fully enjoy it, one most know Hemet, a one-horse desert town on Highway 10, not far from Palm Springs. The first mistake we made was visiting this community in the heat of summer! Poor planning on our part!! We didn't even have a hotel reservation. However, when we wanted to check-in at the only hotel, we were welcomed with questions about which discount cards we had. Between the two of us, we came forward with AAA, AARP, plus many more, all of which together gave us a substantial discount. We quickly computed that they were going to pay us to stay there!

Finally the desk clerk wanted to be sure we knew that breakfast was included!

After dinner at a local dive, it was time to retreat to our room and prepare for our next day visits. We knew about a specific community in Hemet and early the next morning headed in the correct direction, when, lo and behold, what did we see in the horizon? A fairy tale castle complete with turrets, a moat, and drawbridge. Had we made a wrong turn and were arriving in Disneyland? No, we were in the correct place. As we wrote in our second book that included southern California, we fully expected to be greeted by the ambassador to Disneyland himself, the one and only, MICKEY MOUSE! Of course, shortly after the book was published, we received a call from the administrator about how offended they were about the Mickey Mouse comment. They even used the words, "lawyer" and "lawsuit." We also got a few, "I told you so" comments from our husbands but, thankfully, nothing ever came of it.

The research/writing project continued throughout the summer of 1989 and we were then ready for the final edit prior to sending our manuscript to Conari Press in Berkeley, California. Since neither of us were computer geniuses, the task of editing and indexing appeared close to insurmountable, but we attacked it with determination. We picked a day in October when both our husbands were scheduled to be out of town and vowed to start at 7:00 a.m. and work straight through until the final edit was complete. As the afternoon progressed, completion was in sight, but wait! Hold on! It was 5:04 p.m. **The San Francisco Giants** were playing the **Oakland A**s in the World Series.

The Loma Prieta earthquake struck!

We both made a quick run to take cover under Lee Ann's dining room table. In a moment glass from an overturned credenza came down, starting to surround us. The whole kitchen became a mess. There was catsup all over the place and the dog was missing.

When we had caught our breaths, I— Lee Ann—asked. "Sally, did you SAVE it?"

(I meant everything we had worked on so hard and so long, putting it on the computer.)

My—Sally's—answer: "Oh, no!"

Contributors

Bev and Bob Avery met for the first time on a blind date at Lake Tahoe in 1947. Since then they have enjoyed the outdoors and countryside together. Traveling and seeing the diverse beauty and history of this great country have been one of their favorite pastimes.

Betty Bocks believes that the rest of her life has been without major incidents like the two recorded in this book. She is grateful for her children, grandchildren, and great-grandchildren. For her, there have been many years of joy!

June Clodius tells how her Grandmother's words "But God" have led her through life.

Alan Corney and his wife, Judy, had a somewhat unusual courtship, followed by outdoor pursuits in later years with their two children.

Jerry Daniels reports that, born in the Bronx, he has come a long way to the Saratoga Retirement Community!

Isik Doluca considers herself a very lucky person. She had parents who sent her to schools to learn English (which made her life very colorful.) She believes that she has a wonderful family: her husband and two sons.

Kutlu Enver Doluca had the best of two worlds: an interesting career and a good marriage.

Bill Friedrichs was born and raised in San Francisco. In the summers as a young boy he visited his Grandmother in Hopland, a small town in northern California. What is included in this volume are some of the experiences during those visits.

Sheila Gault had a great career and a good life accompanied by many special memories.

Horace ("Oz") Hayes was born and raised in the San Francisco Bay area. He spent four years at Duke University and three more at Yale. During his 80 years he has owned homes in San Francisco, Mill Valley, Sausalito, Los Altos, and Saratoga.

Jim Kistler and his wife, Rita, started a new geological career after their Air Force adventures. This time it was exploring for oil with Chevron. They took their children and lived in various areas ranging from California to Alaska, to London, England, Washington state, and back home again in San Francisco.

Alfreda Mastman would like to be thought of as a very caring and kind person. She prides herself on having many good friends who come from all races and religions and advises her grandchildren to do whatever they can to help create peace in the world.

Barbara Merrill was born and raised in New York City. After college, she worked there, then lived overseas for a period of time, and returned to work again in the city. In 1970 she married John Francis Merrill and three years later they moved to California where they raised a foster child and continued a rich life of joy and excitement together for forty years until his passing in 2010. Living at the Saratoga Retirement Community since March of 2009, she is still working, volunteering, and continuing the kind of life her husband would have wanted for her.

Judith Oppenheimer is a pediatrician who retired in 1998 after being in practice in East San José for 24 years. She is one of the original members of a poetry group, *The Peerless Poets,* who meet weekly to write and gently critique each other's poems. Her poems have been published in a literary journal and three anthologies compiled from readings at the Willow Glen Public Library. Her autobiography, *From Deedle to Dr. Judy: A Memoir of Metamorphosis,* has been published.

Jocelyn Orr reminds the reader that **"Radio Days"** was an entertaining Woody Allen movie set in Queens, New York City. Part of the plot involved the Golden Age of Radio in the early 1940s. Jocelyn's personal radio days occurred during the same time period and in two different social settings: primitive rural west vs. urban east coast.

John Eric Price grew up in England and came to the United States in 1960. He now realizes that much of his life was but a preface to the formation years he has spent at SRC.

Sally Ravel and Lee Ann Wolfe compiled and wrote *Best Retirement Residences in California and the West.* They devoted several years to researching, compiling, and editing the various life styles from which older folks could choose. While the books were directories, they offered pertinent information about neighborhoods, staffing, services, and frequently the writers' own opinions of the community. The authors still get calls to update the information and inquiries from the children of the families they helped years ago.

Richard Roof had the good fortune of spending his summers on a family farm in a small village in Michigan where he collected butterflies, insects, snails, and clams and learned farming tasks ranging from plowing, farm machinery repair, orchard keeping, to beekeeping.

Don Schmidek had a rude awakening during his pre-teen and teen years, compliments of World War II. This was followed by a sad post-war period when the losses of family members took place, as well as those of family possessions and the inability to return to what they considered to be their homeland. His family established a new life in the United States, with good education and occupational growth combined with a loving and patient spouse, great children, and grandchildren. The final transition to SRC was an appropriate culmination.

Joanna Szybalski remarks with pleasure that her poem *"Da Ultima Yoke"* arose from her Norwegian roots. (Both her mother's parents came from Norway.) She does not devalue her inheritance in any way but, rather, enjoys it as much today as she did as a child.

Esther Wedner is almost as proud of her New Orleans origin as she is of being a practicing Jew.

James ("Jim") White, son of a rural fuel oil truck driver and a normal (two-year teachers') school graduate, grew up in the working class section of Ann Arbor, Michigan. His parents never left the state, but as a young man with a frugal and friendly nature and a desire to see life beyond the United States, he traveled twice around the world.

Lou Yabroff went from teaching Home Economics to organizing 103 Try-Y girls' clubs for the YMCA to raising two boys, as well as copying floppy disks in their basement for East Ware Software, Inc., a startup of which she and her husband were one of four founders.